Career Planning and Talent Management

Module 9

ASTD Press is an internationally renowned source of insightful and practical information on workplace learning and performance topics, including training basics, evaluation and return-on-investment (ROI), instructional systems development (ISD), e-learning, leadership, and career development.

Ordering information: This ASTD Learning System and other books published by ASTD Press can be purchased by visiting our Website at store.astd.org or by calling 800.628.2783 or 703.683.8100.
.

Library of Congress Control Number: 2006920964

ISBN-10: 1-56286-447-5

ISBN-13: 978-1-56286-447-7

ASTD Press Staff
Director: Cat Russo
Manager: Mark Morrow
Associate Editor: Tora Estep
Associate Editor: Jennifer Mitchell
Circulation Manager: Marnee Beck
Editorial Assistant: Kelly Norris
Bookstore and Inventory: Nancy Silva
Marketing Manager: Greg Akroyd
Production Coordinator: Rachel Beuter
Cover Design: Alizah Epstein

Printed by Victor Graphics, Baltimore, Maryland, www.victorgraphics.com.

Table of Contents

1
Workforce Planning Approaches

In today's workforce, the environment is constantly changing. Workforce planning is the process and activities that ensure an organization can meet its goals and objectives within this evolving environment. In other words, it ensures the right numbers of the right kinds of people are available at the right times and in the right place.

Workforce planning involves analysis of an organization's human resource (HR) needs, evaluation of its assets, and proactive implementation of strategies. Therefore, career planning (workforce planning for individuals) and talent management (workforce planning for an organization) experts should be aware of the process and outcomes.

Practitioners should be able to explain the definition and components of workforce planning. For example, workforce planning experts should have the skills to analyze HR needs and the internal and external environments of an organization using various quantitative (employee statistics, national and regional statistics, and survey data) or qualitative (interview results, employee assessments, and organization's expectations) methods, as well as produce strategic planning reports.

Learning Objectives:

- ☑ Summarize the relationship between workforce planning and strategic planning.
- ☑ Define the role of HR in workforce planning.
- ☑ List the roles of the workplace learning and performance professional in the organization.
- ☑ Describe the workforce planning process, including the methods and types of data used.

Relationship Between Strategic Planning and Workforce Planning

Strategic planning is a process of systematically organizing the future—a process in which *human resource development (HRD)* managers use past experience as a base for future decisions. Strategic planning is designed to help practitioners focus their attention on an organization's desired outcomes. The process consists of the following seven separate, but interrelated steps:

1. Identification of organizational values (see Chapter 3)

2. Creation of an operational mission statement

3. Environmental analysis (internal and external) (see Chapter 3)

4. Identification of the organization's goals and objectives

5. Identification of action steps designed to accomplish the plan

6. Reality testing the plan

7. Feedback.

Strategic planning, as much a philosophy as a plan, should be used as a tool to enable managers to accomplish more of the things critical to the training function and the HRD process. For that reason, strategic planning should not be a one-time effort, but an ongoing event. Finally, strategic planning should help integrate the HRD program into the organization.

The *workforce plan*—which identifies skill and knowledge gaps and the skills and knowledge required to meet future workforce needs—emanates from the strategic plan. In general, a workforce plan provides managers with a framework for making staffing decisions based on an organization's mission, strategic plan, budgetary resources, and set of desired competencies.

Role of HR in Workforce Planning

The professional field of HRD encompasses education, training, employee development, management development, executive and leadership development, organization development, human performance technology, and organizational learning. The purpose is to improve performance by developing human expertise through organization development and training and development.

Succession Planning

With regard to workforce planning, HRD professionals forecast an organization's human and capital needs. Part of the workforce plan is a succession plan, which helps an organization strategically and proactively plan for replacement personnel.

Succession planning helps organizations survive and thrive in a business world filled with outsourcing, work elimination, business-process-improvement initiatives, and restructuring.

Business has moved from an industrial economy to a knowledge economy. Knowledge has expanded through technology, powerful information systems, and virtual teams communicating via email and the Internet.

The focus is on creating a self-reliant workforce in which employees take advantage of opportunities offered to build valuable skills, enhance employability, and prepare for the rapidly shifting future. In exchange, companies gain increased productivity, a pool of developed talent, and some degree of commitment while the employee works there.

Many progressive companies provide internal career centers or support external centers that have resources and counselors to support their employees in managing their own careers.

Roles of Workplace Learning and Performance Professionals in Organizations

The ASTD Models of HRD (1989) study results, compiled after numerous meetings and several rounds of questionnaires to more than 800 experts in the HRD field, were published in five volumes. As a result of this initiative, HRD was defined as the integrated use of training and development, organization development, and career development to improve individual, group, and organizational effectiveness. Those training and development, organization development, and career development use development as their primary process, and are the focal point of this study. HRD was placed in the larger context of a human resource wheel, as illustrated in Figure 1-1. This model lists 11 HRD roles, 35 competencies, and 74 work outputs.

Workforce Planning Processes

The HRD process, according to Scott (2000), includes a series of seven steps. These steps include:

1. ***Understanding the business context:*** Workplace learning and performance (WLP) professionals review the corporate vision, mission, and strategy and conduct an external analysis. This information then is linked to critical business issues.

2. ***Envisioning future needs:*** WLP professionals determine future business needs (in terms of performance productivity, critical issues, and process improvements) and future career development needs (in terms of competency modes: knowledge, skills, attitudes, outputs/tasks).

3. ***Assessing current realities:*** Practitioners determine business performance by mapping the as-is process, as well as using benchmarking and statistical data analysis, and determine individual competencies via self-assessment, peer assessment, manager assessment, and subordinate assessment. This also may involve researching current workforce data from the Department of Labor and Labor Statistics.

Figure 1-1. The Human Resource Wheel

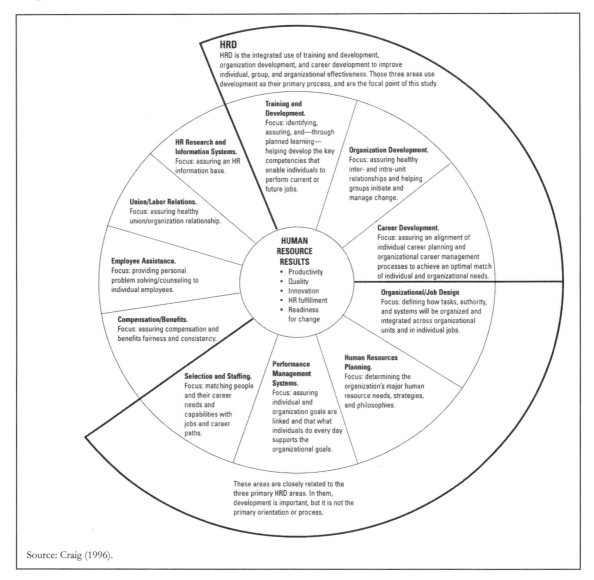

HRD
HRD is the integrated use of training and development, organization development, and career development to improve individual, group, and organizational effectiveness. Those three areas use development as their primary process, and are the focal point of this study.

Training and Development. Focus: identifying, assuring, and—through planned learning—helping develop the key competencies that enable individuals to perform current or future jobs.

HR Research and Information Systems. Focus: assuring an HR information base.

Organization Development. Focus: assuring healthy inter- and intra-unit relationships and helping groups initiate and manage change.

Union/Labor Relations. Focus: assuring healthy union/organization relationship.

Career Development. Focus: assuring an alignment of individual career planning and organizational career management processes to achieve an optimal match of individual and organizational needs.

HUMAN RESOURCE RESULTS
• Productivity
• Quality
• Innovation
• HR fulfillment
• Readiness for change

Employee Assistance. Focus: providing personal problem solving/counseling to individual employees.

Organizational/Job Design Focus: defining how tasks, authority, and systems will be organized and integrated across organizational units and in individual jobs.

Compensation/Benefits. Focus: assuring compensation and benefits fairness and consistency.

Human Resources Planning. Focus: determining the organization's major human resource needs, strategies, and philosophies.

Selection and Staffing. Focus: matching people and their career needs and capabilities with jobs and career paths.

Performance Management Systems. Focus: assuring individual and organization goals are linked and that what individuals do every day supports the organizational goals.

These areas are closely related to the three primary HRD areas. In them, development is important, but it is not the primary orientation or process.

Source: Craig (1996).

4. ***Analyzing the gaps:*** WLP professionals compare future needs with current realities to determine gaps and prioritize results. This step focuses on determining if the gaps are causing staffing, financial, and organizational problems due to a skill deficiency. In this step, practitioners identify the competencies needed and the number of positions required in the next five to 20 years. They may conduct workforce surveys and analyze trends and forecasts in alignment with the strategic plan.

5. ***Designing the learning strategy:*** Practitioners determine learning objectives and best-practice methods, tie the learning strategies to competencies and issues, and implement best-practice learning (just-in-time, applied, modular, and so forth).

6. **_Evaluating and measuring:_** Once employees take the required learning and follow-up activities occur, WLP professionals determine if the learning addressed the skill or knowledge gaps. An organization may implement Kirkpatrick's four levels of evaluation or another method to evaluate the success of the learning.

7. **_Improving continually:_** Practitioners institute or review ongoing processes to improve design and delivery, increase the use of learning on the job, and help employees make informed decisions.

✓ Chapter 1 Knowledge Check

1. Which of the following best defines strategic planning?

    a. A process of surveying employees for the purpose of developing reward and recognition systems

    b. A process of systematically organizing the future

    c. A process of facilitating group brainstorming and gathering knowledge-management data

    d. A process of identifying performance gaps and selecting appropriate learning interventions

2. Which of the following best describes a subset of the correct strategic planning steps in the correct order?

    a. Identification of organizational values, environmental analysis, identification of the organization's goals and objectives, identification of action steps designed to accomplish the plan

    b. Environmental analysis, identification of the organization's goals and objectives, identification of action steps designed to accomplish the plan

    c. Identification of the organization's goals and objectives, environmental analysis, identification of organizational values, identification of action steps designed to accomplish the plan

    d. Identification of action steps designed to accomplish the plan, identification of organizational values, environmental analysis, identification of the organization's goals and objectives

3. Workforce planning processes include which of the following steps?

    a. Understand the business context, assess current realities, develop a strategic plan

    b. Understand the business context, assess current realities, analyze gaps

    c. Envision future needs, assess current realities, develop a strategic plan

    d. Analyze gaps, design learning instruction, implement instruction

4. Which of the following is not true?

    a. Strategic plans should be used as a tool to enable managers to accomplish more of the things that are critical to the training function.

    b. Strategic planning is a process of systematically organizing the future—a process in which past experience is used to make future decisions.

    c. Strategic planning should integrate the HRD program into the organization.

    d. Strategic planning identifies skill and knowledge gaps and the skills and knowledge required to meet future workforce needs.

5. A workforce plan identifies

    a. The skill and knowledge gaps and skills and knowledge required to meet future needs

    b. The number of resources required to meet future needs

    c. The future roles and responsibilities of a job

    d. The best candidates with potential to move into a new job

6. Which of the following workforce planning processes is best described as determining future needs (performance, productivity, critical issues, and process improvements)?

    a. Understanding the business content

    b. Envisioning future needs

    c. Assessing current realities

    d. Analyzing gaps

References

Buckner, M., and L. Slavenski. (1993). "Succession Planning." *Infoline* No. 259312.

Craig, R.L., ed. (1996). *The ASTD Training and Development Handbook.* New York: McGraw-Hill.

Gilley, J.W. (1992). "Strategic Planning for Human Resource Development." *Infoline* No. 259206.

McLagan, P.A. (1989). *The Models.* Alexandria, VA: ASTD.

Rothwell, W. (1996). "Selecting and Developing the Professional Human Resource Staff." In Robert L. Craig, ed., *The ASTD Training and Development Handbook.* New York: McGraw-Hill.

Scott, B. (2000). *Consulting on the Inside.* Alexandria, VA: ASTD Press.

2
Succession and Replacement Planning Approaches

Succession planning and replacement planning, simply put, are processes to ensure the continuity of key leadership positions and the stability of tenure of an organization's personnel. Unlike replacement planning, which can be described as a type of risk management, succession planning is defined as a means of identifying critical management positions, starting at the project manager and supervisor levels and extending up to the highest organizational positions. Succession planning also helps provide maximum flexibility in lateral management moves to ensure that as individuals achieve greater seniority, their management skills will broaden.

Succession planning or replacement planning should be carefully developed and implemented in organizations according to their characteristics and environment. Therefore, as experts in this area, WLP professionals should be aware of the types of approaches they can apply, as well as the general definitions and processes of succession planning and replacement planning.

Learning Objectives:

- ☑ Define succession planning and explain the differences between succession planning and replacement planning.
- ☑ List and describe six approaches to strategic plan integration and succession planning.
- ☑ List and describe three traditional and three alternative job movement approaches.
- ☑ Detail the succession planning process and explain how competency modeling, needs assessment procedures, and evaluation of employees fit into the process.

Definition of Succession Planning

In today's dynamic world of mergers, acquisitions, downsizings, shrinking markets, and flattening organizations, many companies are asking two key questions about succession planning:

- Do we have qualified people ready to fill key positions now and grow the business in the next three to five years? (This is the short-term emphasis.)

- Will we have a sufficient number of qualified candidates ready in five to 10 years to fill key positions? (This is the long-term emphasis.)

Because constantly evolving environments challenge many organizations, the implementation of a succession planning program requires the use of change-management strategies. It is well known that changing organizations succeed by having the right people in the right places at the right times.

Designing a successful succession planning program is not accomplished by copying another organization's plan. Developing a succession plan is accomplished by asking questions that pertain to the specific issues of a changing organization now and continuing to ask those questions as the organization progresses through the inevitable transformations.

Succession planning entails the identification of employees who have the right skills to meet challenges the organization faces. During this process, the WLP professional

- identifies and analyzes key positions

- assesses candidates against job and personal requirements

- creates individual development plans

- selects people for certain roles.

Succession planning is a long-term strategic initiative that ensures that the right staff are in the right jobs at the right times. The process also ensures the continued effective performance of an organization by establishing a way to develop and replace key staff over time.

Succession planning normally focuses on identifying replacements for specific top positions. In some cases where a number of people can fill certain positions (for example, general managers, business leaders, or domestic or international representatives), organizations use a group approach. In this situation, a group of individuals is groomed to fill any number of similar positions.

Succession planning is used to help organizations solve business problems, such as the following:

- Who will move into this key financial position when Ron retires?

- In view of our vulnerable domestic situation, who can be spared to open the new European market?

- We have three positions open. Pat will move into one. How do we fill the other two?

- Why aren't more female and minority employees in the executive suite?

- Joan is not quite ready for this assignment, but if we hire externally, will we lose her?

- How can we keep John from leaving us? He is a key player.

If an organization raises questions such as these and finds no ready answers or solutions, it is possibly time to develop and implement a succession planning process. This process will help ensure leadership continuity. Obviously, every organization needs to develop its own culture-sensitive system. Although no one system fits all, the general process outlined in the "Succession Planning Processes" section later in this chapter can be applied when embarking on this process.

Organizations that carry out succession planning correctly will have fully prepared frontline and management staff to step into positions left vacant due to retirement and general attrition.

Practitioners must not confuse succession planning with replacement hiring, which commonly happens. Replacement hiring is just that: "We've got to replace her right away, so let's fill this position now!" Notice the urgency in that decision? This is exactly what organizations need to avoid.

Succession planning means continually striving to identify and develop talent that will carry the organization's strategic planning into the next generation of leadership. Succession planning ensures continuity for leadership in all positions, rather than just quickly replacing an employee or filling an open position. Table 2-1 outlines the key differences between replacement hiring and succession planning.

Table 2-1. Key Differences Between Replacement Hiring and Succession Planning

Replacement Hiring Is...	Succession Planning Is...
Reacting to fill a position fast	Being proactive and planning in advance who will step in to fill a vacancy
A narrow and temporary approach to filling a position	In sync with the organization's overall strategic plan and goals
A substitution	A renewed commitment
An attempt to head off a crisis and to cope	Long-term talent building
Inflexibility	Flexibility
Hiring the best of what's available	Hiring the best

Job Movement and Replacement Approaches

Within organizations, there are many traditional and alternative job movement and replacement approaches. Table 2-2 summarizes these approaches.

Table 2-2. Traditional and Alternative Job Movement and Replacement Approaches

Traditional Approaches	Alternative Approaches
In (entry)	Process redesign
Out (termination)	Outsourcing
Up (promotion)	Talent pools
Down (demotion)	Competitive skill inventories
Across (lateral)	Temping
Progress in place (development in current position)	Job sharing
	Part-time employment
	Consulting
	Overtime
	Job rotation
	Retirees

Approaches to Strategic Plan Integration and Succession Planning

The primary component of a succession planning system is the identification of replacement personnel. At its simplest, this requires a statement of who will fill a given job when it becomes vacant. At its best, *succession planning* includes an evaluation of the quality and readiness of the named successors.

When conducting succession planning, there are several approaches and tips that organizations can leverage including:

- *Top-down:* In this approach, individuals or a pool of resources are identified by top management. Managers or a panel of managers can recommend and evaluate individuals.

- *Market-driven:* In this approach, succession planning is a function of marketplace need. Talent is acquired as competition and marketplace conditions require.

- *Career-planning:* In this approach, succession planning is part of workers' career planning. Based on the organizational strategy and plans, individuals make career decisions, along with their managers and others.

- *Future-oriented:* In this approach, management anticipates future competitive and marketplace challenges and adjusts talent to meet anticipated conditions.

- *Bottom-up:* In this approach, managers make initial recommendations as to who can be replacements for their direct reports.

- *Combination:* The approaches listed previously can be combined to meet the needs of the organization.

Succession Planning Processes

This section presents a four-phased succession planning model that covers establishing the scope of the plan; creating the plan; implementing the plan; and monitoring, evaluating, and revising the plan. One important element that should run through all phases of succession planning is communication with staff to stop the rumor mill and prevent formation of misperceptions and anxieties. Another important element to consider when initiating and implementing a succession planning program is the ethical and legal considerations, which are detailed further in Chapter 6.

Phase 1. Establish the Scope

Generally, the HR department leads a succession planning effort with key staff input. The steps involved in establishing the scope of the succession plan include

- reviewing the organization's strategic plan

- analyzing attrition data and retirement projections

- identifying external factors

- defining plan parameters.

Reviewing the Strategic Plan

Succession planning builds on an organization's strategic plan, which outlines how the organization reaches the measurable goals and objectives supporting its mission and vision. The strategic plan shapes strategy with information from customers, aligns employees' behavior with the organization's mission, and turns employees' intentions into actions.

Practitioners should review the strategic plan to identify current and future organizational priorities. These priorities determine how staff is distributed across departments and divisions, how functional responsibilities are defined, and how technology is created to support delivery of the organization's products and services. Practitioners need to understand these priorities to identify where retirement and general attrition will have the greatest impact on the organization.

Analyzing the Data

Succession planning requires analysis of retirement projections, attrition patterns, and the anticipated effects of retirement and attrition.

With regard to retirement projections, practitioners should gather information to determine the number of employees (executive, management, and front line) who are eligible for retirement. To begin, they should assess the vulnerability of each department or division to brain drain. This is an example of an assessment:

- In the workforce development department, one of three is 50+ years old (33 percent).

- In sales, three of seven are 40+ years old (43 percent).

Then, practitioners need to determine how many individuals have been identified that may retire in the next five, 10, and 15 years by reviewing the eligibility requirements of the organization's retirement plans.

The next step is analyzing the current attrition patterns to make projections. The following statistical data must be gathered—for the past one to five years—and broken down by age, education level, and gender:

- number of current employees

- number of new hires

- number of voluntary separations (for example, other employment, retirement, or personal)

- number of involuntary separations (for example, terminations)

- other separations (for example, disability, or death)

- average length of employment

- turnover rate

- reasons for attrition.

To determine the effect of retirement and attrition on the organization, several questions related to short- and long-term strategic planning need to be answered, such as:

- Which factors (for example, cost of healthcare) could change attrition patterns?

- Does the organization have qualified people ready to fill key positions in the next three to five years?

- Will the organization have a sufficient number of qualified candidates ready to fill key positions in five to 10 years?

Identifying External Factors

In this step of the succession planning process, external factors that affect staffing levels are assessed. The goal is to determine how to focus the succession planning efforts given the context in which retirement and staff replacement are taking place.

To understand the context, practitioners should take the following steps:

1. Review the organization's strategic plan and annual report.

2. Form a research team and ask each team member to research specific questions.

3. Meet with key people to obtain information and their perspectives on the future of the workforce and the organization.

4. Ask staff to interview individuals they know in professional organizations for information that might be useful.

5. Benchmark practices against other organizations to determine best practices.

6. Conduct informational interviews with the organization's executives to get their perspectives on what it takes to keep their positions.

Defining Parameters

Defining plan parameters ensures that goals can be accomplished in given timeframes. The time to implement changes also influences the choice of scope.

Phase 2. Create the Plan

The steps involved in creating the succession plan include

- identifying job functions (see Chapter 3)

- identifying staffing levels needed and related to *knowledge, skills,* and *attitudes (KSAs)*

- determining staff availability

- conducting gap analysis and establishing priorities

- developing a workforce plan that includes measures of success.

Identifying Job Functions

Job functions are major responsibilities of programs or departments that have specific outputs and outcomes for internal and external clients. Given the scope of the succession plan, practitioners identify which functions will need to be staffed, considering existing functions as well as potential future functions.

Identifying Staffing Levels and KSAs

Once the important functions have been identified with regard to the succession plan, practitioners determine staffing needs by identifying critical KSAs and the number of staff needed with each KSA or competency set.

At this point, practitioners may use competency modeling as one of the techniques in succession planning. Competency models provide a unifying framework among the different HR functions and a broad overview of the capabilities required to perform successfully within an organization.

Over the years, management experts and researchers have compiled lists of critical competencies for excellent managers. Although the lists change from time to time and from company to company, their basic components remain consistent: identify competencies or KSAs and managers' needs and then build the organization's management responsibilities around those competencies.

KSA Definitions

- *Knowledge* involves the development of intellectual skills. Examples of knowledge include understanding the principles of engineering, how to organize plants in a garden, or knowing how to complete a series of steps to complete a task or process.

- *Skill* refers to physical movement, coordination, and the use of motor skills to accomplish a task. An example of skills is the ability to operate a piece of equipment.

- *Attitude* refers to how people deal with things emotionally, such as feelings, motivations, and enthusiasm.

Depth of knowledge and breadth of skill vary from one managerial level to another. Practitioners need to go beyond the identification of general competencies to their specific applications at various managerial levels. The competencies required for first-level supervisors differ from those for middle-level managers, just as the competencies required for executive officers differ from those for middle managers.

A task analysis is an efficient method to determine what competencies managers should have. Chapter 3 describes job and task analysis in greater detail.

Determining Staff Availability

In this step of succession planning, practitioners determine how many staff will be available after the anticipated attrition of the target population and assess the competency of remaining employees.

Calculating staff supply is a three-step process:

1. The number of employees currently employed is calculated and grouped into these categories: title, grade, organization, location, skills or competencies, or other.

2. The attrition pattern is calculated by adding up the number of employees who might retire, die, transfer, or obtain an interdepartmental promotion by title, grade, organization, location, skills or competencies, and other.

3. The projected workforce based on expected attrition without hiring replacements is described.

After determining what the staff supply is likely to be, a practitioner identifies remaining employees with the skills to replace departing staff members.

Analyzing Gaps and Priorities

A practitioner should conduct a gap analysis to determine the skill gap for each job title. This process may leverage several needs assessment procedures, as well as performance management concepts.

Creating the Workforce Plan

After job functions have been prioritized, a practitioner should create solutions to staffing shortages. This can be accomplished by developing implementation strategies and measurements for each goal and objective in the plan. To develop strategies for each goal, practitioners may research best practices of other organizations, brainstorm potential solutions, and then narrow the list by evaluating the pros and cons of each option. A practitioner should also identify barriers to implementation and make recommendations to eliminate those barriers.

Phase 3. Implement the Plan

In the implementation phase, practitioners communicate the succession planning process and implementation strategies. Because communication of a major initiative can define its success, sharing information about the plan is critical before, during, and after implementation.

It also is important to remember that employees determine the significance of an initiative by evaluating the communication with which it is associated. To emphasize the importance of the initiative, a practitioner should create a communication plan that ensures continued, visible information about the status of the strategic planning effort. When rolling out the succession plan, a practitioner should

- get sponsorship from executives
- update the management teams
- implement capacity-building efforts
- create effective transfer strategies
- engage stakeholders
- anticipate staff reactions
- get naysayers on board.

Phase 4. Monitor, Evaluate, and Revise

Once the succession plan has been implemented, the practitioner monitors progress, evaluates implementation, and revises the plan as needed.

At this point, employees are evaluated to identify candidates for future roles. The performance appraisal and *360-degree evaluation* processes will help practitioners identify current KSAs and determine future learning interventions to develop employees in other competency areas.

Employees identified as potential candidates for future job roles should have learning interventions incorporated into their ***individual development plans (IDPs)*** as part of the succession planning program.

Because succession planning will become an ongoing part of the organization's business plan, evaluating the effectiveness of the succession plan and making revisions as appropriate will be necessary.

Evaluation Models and Procedures

Practitioners should be familiar with the most common models and procedures to evaluate the success of HRD programs and how they might be applied to determine if goals were met and planned measurable results achieved. These models include

- Kirkpatrick's four levels of evaluation

- the return-on-investment (ROI) model

- the balanced scorecard model.

More information on these evaluation models is provided in Module 4, *Measuring and Evaluating.*

✓ Chapter 2 Knowledge Check

1. A key difference between succession planning and replacement hiring is that succession planning is proactive and focuses on future needs, whereas replacement hiring is reactive to fill current positions.

   a. True

   b. False

2. Which of the following is not one of the approaches to replacement and succession planning?

   a. Top down

   b. Future oriented

   c. Promoting

   d. Market driven

3. Which of the following is an example of an alternative job movement approach?

   a. Entry into the organization

   b. Termination

   c. Promotion

   d. Outsourcing

4. Which of the following best describes competency modeling?

   a. Identifying critical KSAs based on lists compiled by experts to identify the knowledge and breadth of skill that various managerial roles in the organization need

   b. Calculating the number of employees currently employed and grouping them by categories such as title, grade, location, and skills

   c. Analyzing gaps and priorities for each job title to determine the existence or extent of a skill gap

   d. Creating a workforce plan that addresses staffing shortages

5. Which of the following is not a step in the succession planning process?

   a. Defining plan parameters

   b. Reviewing organizational strategic plans

   c. Reacting quickly to fill vacant positions

   d. Analyzing attrition data and retirement projects

References

Bruce, A. (2001). *Leaders—Start to Finish*. Alexandria, VA: ASTD Press.

Buckner, M., and L. Slavenski. (1993). "Succession Planning." *Infoline* No. 259312.

Hastings, S. (2004). "Succession Planning: Take Two." *Infoline* No. 250405.

Rothwell, W.J. (2000). *Effective Succession Planning*. 2nd edition. New York: AMACOM.

Russell, S. (1987). "The Management Development Process." *Infoline* No. 258711.

Sonnenfeld, J. (1988). *The Hero's Farewell*. New York: Oxford University Press.

3
Job Analysis Tools and Procedures

Job analysis is the process used to break a job into its component duty or functional areas and the task statements associated with those duty areas. The key deliverable of the job analysis is a validated task list. This task list is a critical deliverable because it can be used as the foundation to create multiple derivative products, including curriculum design, behavioral interview guides, self-assessment tools, organizational assessments, job descriptions, and competency models.

A variety of techniques, methods, and tools are available to conduct a job analysis. In many cases, the HR department's compensation unit has developed standard procedures for these analyses. Knowledge of the job analysis process and the various methods and tools used can facilitate the career planning and talent management processes by identifying the knowledge, skills, abilities, work behaviors, and education required for various jobs within a career path. This knowledge can help an organization identify and improve its talent force.

The key for the WLP professional is to understand the job analysis process. That way he or she can help people identify the skills, knowledge, abilities, work behaviors, and education that are crucial for developing their careers and preparing for specific jobs within that career. Generally, an HR compensation specialist handles the major responsibility for this area. However, it is important for the WLP professional to work closely with the compensation expert and understand which methods are most appropriate for the various jobs.

Learning Objectives:

- ☑ Discuss two data-collection techniques used during job analysis.
- ☑ List three types of analyses that should be conducted prior to conducting a job analysis.
- ☑ List six job analysis methods and briefly describe the benefits and constraints of each.
- ☑ Discuss the advantages and disadvantages of task analysis, gap analysis, performance analysis, competency assessment, and content analysis.
- ☑ Describe how the outcomes of the analysis can be used in training delivery and at the conclusion of a job analysis.

Job Analysis Overview

Job analysis is an important to the WLP practitioner. The process is crucial in helping individuals develop their careers and in helping organizations develop employees and maximize their talent. The outcomes of job analysis are key drivers in designing learning, as well as valuable aids for improving processes and analyzing the value of certain job positions.

These are some typical tasks in the job analysis process:

- creating new-hire training

- developing behavior-based interview questions

- writing performance objectives

- helping employees prepare for the next job level.

The information gathered from a job analysis can be used to identify skill gaps and to develop an IDP for improvement in the current job or job advancement. The plan may or may not be tied to a performance appraisal system; however, a good plan usually is integrated with a performance appraisal.

A job analysis is more detailed than a job description and less detailed than a task analysis. *Job descriptions* generally explain the duties of a job, but do not get into the specific tasks necessary to fulfill the stated duties. A *task analysis,* however, examines a single task within a job and breaks it down into the actual steps of performance. While task analysis is about the *how* of a job, job analysis is focused on the *what*.

Job analysis identifies all duties and the respective tasks done on a daily, weekly, monthly, and yearly basis that make up a single job function. A thorough job analysis results in a complete picture of the job, including

- duties

- tasks, ranked by select factors

- general knowledge and skills required to be successful

- resources needed to perform the job effectively.

A complete job analysis can take the form of a map—and it functions exactly like that—a map to approach whatever goal the employee must achieve. How one applies the results varies based on the organizational demands. Several methods of conducting job analyses will be discussed later in this section.

Data-Collection Techniques

Various data-collection instruments and techniques may be used to gather the needed information, including interviews, surveys, focus groups, and corrective action reports. The choice of method depends on the number of people in the targeted performance group and how many people are affected by the performers.

The need for accurate information is critical in the HR and performance training areas to

- determine the current skill levels
- identify optimal performance levels and performance gaps
- conduct needs and training requirements analyses
- determine which intervention provides the required learning.

Before collecting data, a practitioner needs to determine whether any external definitions and standards exist for a particular question. For example, local unemployment figures may list clerical help as typists, stenographers, and secretaries, whereas an HRD specialists' organization may use titles such as word processor, secretary, and administrative assistant. In this situation, a difference in definition can skew the analysis of the data collected.

Pre-Job Analysis

Prior to conducting a job analysis, practitioners may conduct other types of analyses, including

- *Organization analysis*: Important organization values directly influence how people behave. During organization analysis, HRD practitioners identify the feelings, beliefs, and attitudes of employees, as well as the organization's decision makers. The composite of these values makes up the organizational culture.

- *Cost-benefit analysis:* This type of ROI analysis is used to prove that an intervention either paid for itself or generated more financial benefit than costs.

- *Audience analysis:* This analysis is conducted to understand the target population, demographics, and other relevant information prior to job analysis, training, or other solution.

- *Environmental analysis:* This helps establish a strategic plan for HRD programs and helps practitioners determine organizational strengths and weaknesses (internal) and opportunities and threats (external). Internal environmental analysis considers the organization's financial condition, managers' abilities and attitudes, facilities, staffing size and quality, competitive position, image, and structure. External environmental analysis considers the organization's economic condition, legal and political realities, social and cultural values, the state of technology, the availability of resources, and the organization's competitive structure.

Job Analysis Methods

A job analysis can be completed using several methods. The method selected depends on the amount of time, access to subject matter experts (SMEs), and the level of detail needed. Coordination with HR ensures job specifications and job descriptions adequately spell out job duties and responsibilities. These are some job analysis methods:

- *Interview:* The interview involves a series of questions to uncover what a person does on the job. The WLP professional generally conducts an interview one-on-one with the performers and supervisors. The primary drawback of using an interview is that a person may have difficulty recalling everything he or she does. However, an interview may be a good method if only a high-level overview of a job and not the task detail is needed. An interview is best when predetermined questions are available, and it is especially useful for professional jobs.

- *Survey or questionnaire:* A written instrument has limitations, primarily because it is cumbersome to fill out in great detail. However, if a general overview of a job is all that's required, this may be an option to consider. An open-ended questionnaire should be used when input is needed from employees and managers. This type of questionnaire is best to use when a large number of jobs must be analyzed. When job analysis is conducted using a computer model, a highly structured questionnaire is strongly recommended. Off-the-shelf surveys that can be distributed to performers are available online.

- *Observation:* This approach involves sitting with the job performer and observing or recording all of the tasks as they are completed. Observation is used to provide a realistic view of daily activities. Observation can be time consuming because job performers rarely perform every task in their job description in the span of one day—so this method is best for short-cycle jobs in production. Also, the presence of an observer can sometimes skew behavior. The benefit of this method is that the analyst will have first-hand knowledge of the tasks performed and can ask questions along the way. But because the focus of a job analysis is primarily on the what of a job, observation is probably best suited for task analysis.

- *Focus group:* This approach involves a group of performers in a specific job function who come together to brainstorm all of the duties and tasks of their job. It is essentially a big group interview. A focus group allows participants to use each other as sounding boards to generate the task list. It is efficient time-wise because the group can collectively think of all the tasks performed on the job on the spot, instead of an analyst observing tasks as time allows.

- *Work diary or log:* Although this method can be used for most jobs, a diary or a log often provides too much data and is difficult to interpret.

When beginning a job analysis, practitioners need to be sure to coordinate with the HR department to ensure that job descriptions and job specifications adequately spell out duties and responsibilities.

Types of Job Analysis: Advantages and Disadvantages

Before getting into the details of conducting a job analysis, it's necessary to understand the key terms and concepts associated with the process. Job analysis identifies the duties and tasks that make up a single job function. It may be helpful to think of a *job* as the 20,000-

foot level, *tasks* as the 5,000-foot level, and individual *steps* taken within each task as at sea level.

Task Analysis

Task analysis seeks to identify the knowledge and skills necessary to do a job. A task

- has a beginning and an end
- consists of two or more steps
- results in a specific, measurable output (either a decision, product, or service)
- can be performed independently of other tasks.

A job can have many tasks. The amount of task information to capture in a job analysis depends on the business needs. The WLP professional may elect to capture tasks down to the administration level (such as, make copies) or choose to focus on meatier tasks (such as, analyze and interpret the weekly sales numbers) that represent the bulk of the job in question.

The advantage of a task analysis is that it makes note of the minute details of the specific tasks required of a job. A disadvantage is that it can be time consuming to collect this detailed data.

Performance Gap Analysis

This process must proceed from macro to micro. That is, beginning with a customer focus that takes into account the context of the marketplace in which the organization, department, or function operates is essential. A *performance gap analysis* identifies and describes past, present, and potential future human performance gaps. A WLP professional should collect information from stakeholders—executives, department heads, line managers, and so forth—as well as individual performers by asking questions that examine how existing performance compares with the desired performance. Then, a WLP professional must examine any documents (such as annual reports or customer surveys) to find the consequences of the performance gap.

Specifically, performance gap analysis should address people because people are the organization. As with any analysis, a variety of methods should be selected to collect the information, including surveys, interviews, and focus groups.

As a result of the performance analysis, the WLP professional should be able to answer the following questions:

- What is the desired performance situation versus the actual situation?
- What is the gap or difference between the actual and desired performance?
- Who is affected by the performance gap?
- When and where did the performance gap first occur, or when is it expected to begin?

- When and where were the symptoms and consequences of the performance gap first noticed?

- What has the performance gap cost the organization? Can the impact of the performance gap be measured?

WLP professionals conduct this analysis to determine the existence or extent of a skill gap for *each* job title. These are three primary types of gaps to look for when performing this analysis:

1. Excess staff performing obsolete or declining functions, or functions that will likely go unchanged

2. Inadequate supply of qualified staff for positions that will likely go unchanged

3. Inadequate supply of staff with needed skill sets for positions that may require a change in classification

The performance gap analysis should define

- the current state

- the desired state

- methods for change to achieve the desired performance.

After analyzing the gaps, a practitioner should consider the direction of the organization to prioritize staff gaps. The overall goal is to discover and define the discrepancy.

The advantage of this type of analysis is that it provides the essential information needed to improve a problem situation. The disadvantage of conducting this analysis is that it can be difficult to discern what it will take to close a performance gap.

Competency Assessment

Every job requires certain skills and knowledge. A job analysis helps practitioners identify the required competencies and categorize jobs according to such requirements. Three competency elements that constitute most positions are

- *managerial or administrative:* skills required to plan, organize, control, manage, and administer functions, processes, projects, departments, and organizations

- *supervisory:* skills required to supervise, direct, lead, counsel, discipline, coach, and develop people

- *functional:* skills or knowledge required to perform specific tasks such as operating a computer, videotaping a seminar, or writing a technical training manual.

Although the elements overlap, practitioners use these to guide skills assessment and determine qualifications for a particular job.

The advantage *and* disadvantage of this analysis is that it is generic enough to be used for several jobs.

Content Analysis

As part of designing learning, WLP practitioners undergo the process of identifying the essential information that learners need to bridge gaps in KSAs. This not only confirms the appropriate content, but also identifies strategies for making the content to be learned more manageable.

This review and categorization of the information to be covered in the learning solutions is called content analysis. Practitioners first identify the whole of the subject matter, select what is relevant to accomplish the instructional goals, and then break down the content into manageable chunks of information and determine the appropriate media to deliver the content.

The advantage of this analysis is that it results in boosted performance and ultimately a better bottom line. The disadvantage is that it is often time-consuming and costly.

Uses of Job Analysis Outcomes

Once the job analysis is complete, practitioners prioritize job titles and functions and create solutions for staffing shortages. Practitioners develop implementation strategies for each identified goal and objective in the form of a project plan. To create the implementation strategies, practitioners need to

- research best practices of other organizations

- familiarize themselves with key topics

- ask for employee input on the identified topics

- brainstorm potential solutions and narrow the list by evaluating the pros and cons of each option

- identify barriers and recommendations to eliminate them.

A practitioner needs to create measures of success for each implementation strategy selected. In this process, a practitioner defines success and determines outcomes that demonstrate attainment of goals by defining the measures for each specific outcome. The practitioner also creates interim measures of success to be used for monitoring progress, as well as final measures of success.

Measures of success are critical because they are used to communicate to staff and executives the value of the work done by the succession planning team. Without clear measures, the WLP professional cannot prove accomplishments and ensure continued support for the team's work.

Other job analysis outcomes need to funnel back into training programs and materials to ensure that the training accurately supports the job tasks and needs. For example, practitioners may need to create criterion-referenced or performance-based assessments to measure a training program's ability to convey new knowledge and skill information, as well as to determine a performer's skills. Practitioners can use job analysis outcomes when determining and selecting the types of intervention strategies, training materials, and activities that will be used to help develop employees. Based on the nature of the tasks, how often they need to be performed, the target employees, and how geographically dispersed the employees are, practitioners also may choose a variety of delivery methods to quickly provide anytime, anywhere information as needed to support on-the-job performance.

✓ Chapter 3 Knowledge Check

1. A job analysis is the process of

    a. Identifying performance gaps and training needs

    b. Breaking a job into its component duty or functional areas

    c. Breaking a task into its sub-tasks to define the job

    d. Identifying standard procedures and process flows

2. Two data-collection techniques used during job analysis are focus groups and corrective action reports.

    a. True

    b. False

3. Which of the following statements is not true?

    a. A task analysis seeks to identify the knowledge and skills necessary to do a job.

    b. A task analysis uses data-collection instruments that are quick and efficient to implement.

    c. A task analysis documents tasks in terms of a specific and measurable output.

    d. A task analysis documents tasks that can be performed independently of other tasks.

4. Which of the following is not usually conducted prior to conducting a job analysis?

    a. Audience analysis

    b. Organization analysis

    c. Environmental analysis

    d. Culture audit

5. Which of the following analysis methods uses a questionnaire, often with open-ended questions, when input is needed from employees and managers?

    a. Interviews

    b. Observation

    c. Surveys

    d. Work diaries

6. Which of the following analysis methods is best used for processes with short-cycle jobs in production due to the time-consuming nature of this method?

    a. Interviews

    b. Observation

    c. Surveys

    d. Work diaries

7. All of the following are examples of job analyses except

   a. Content analysis

   b. Competency assessment

   c. Performance analysis

   d. Compensation analysis

8. All of the following are examples of job analysis outcomes except

   a. Developing strategic plan goals

   b. Prioritizing job titles and functions

   c. Identifying solutions for staffing shortages

   d. Creating measures of success

References

Barksdale, S., and T. Lund. (2001). *Rapid Evaluation*. Alexandria, VA: ASTD Press.

Buckner, M., and L. Slavenski. (1993). "Succession Planning." *Infoline* No. 259312.

Franklin, M. (2005). "A Guide to Job Analysis." *Infoline* No. 250506.

Gilley, J.W. (1992). "Strategic Planning for Human Resource Development." *Infoline* No. 259206.

Hartley, D.E. (September 2004). "Job Analysis at the Speed of Reality." *T+D*, pp. 20-22.

Hastings, S. (2004). "Succession Planning." *Infoline* No. 250405.

Leibowitz, Z.B., A.H. Souerwine, and J.E. McMahon. (1985). "Career Guidance Discussions." *Infoline* No. 258507.

Long, L. (1998). "Surveys From Start to Finish." *Infoline* No. 258612.

Piskurich, G.M. (2002). *HPI Essentials*. Alexandria, VA.: ASTD Press.

Waagen, A.K. (1997). "Essentials for Evaluation." *Infoline* No. 259705.

4

Career Development Theories and Approaches

Career development theories and approaches provide the fundamental basis for individual career development and organizational talent management. This competency provides a conceptual basis that affects workforce planning, talent management, and performance improvement. The competency is broad and covers most other areas within the career planning and talent management area, as it requires the expert to draw or link to other areas, including HR functions and counseling. Experts in this area often have additional competencies related to psychological counseling and human growth and development and consequently are licensed or certified to assess and interpret various psychological career instruments. Experts can identify various theories that are relevant to career development and identify which approaches best apply to the individual or best balance organizational (succession planning) and individual counseling. Professionals must be skilled in interviewing and counseling individual employees, interpret and produce reports based on various psychological instruments, and assist the individual in developing realistic career plans.

Learning Objectives:

☑ Define what is meant by the balance between personal assessment and the market.

☑ Discuss Williamson's trait and factor theory and how it relates to career development.

☑ Define the Ginzberg and Super developmental frameworks.

☑ Summarize each of the personality or typology theories, including Roe's theory, Holland's occupational congruency model, psychodynamic theory, and sociological theory, and compare their value for the individual employee.

☑ Describe Krumboltz's behavioral theory.

☑ Discuss Edgar Schein's career anchors theory.

☑ Describe how gender, culture, and generational issues affect career development.

Balance Between Personal Assessment and the Market

Determining the ideal future of the organization in terms of career development is a process that must be based on appropriate concepts and theories, according to Zandy B. Leibowitz (1986), a career development specialist and author. This "vision must be realistic and provide a strong link between the present situation and future possibilities," including organizational needs and appropriate interventions. Leibowitz suggests a first step of focusing on "real needs, structures, and cultures." Next, vision is established by "gaining a realistic picture of what the organization, its employees, and its managers will look like in five years if the specific needs already identified are truly addressed." Finally, Leibowitz suggests employing career development theories to "provide a sense of direction, a rationale for approaches, and indications upon which to measure results."

Trait and Factor: Williamson's Theory

Trait-and-factor counseling is the traditional approach to career decision making. Although the approach is often criticized, it is widely used throughout the industry. *Trait* refers to a characteristic of an individual that can be measured through testing. *Factor* refers to a characteristic required for successful job performance.

The trait-and-factor approach to counseling is based on the thought that people can be understood in terms of the traits they possess. Traits can include intelligence, ambition, aptitude, and self-esteem. Factors are statistical representations of the traits.

According to Roy H. Tunick, Professor in the Department of Counseling, Rehabilitation Counseling, and Counseling Psychology at West Virginia University College of Human Resources and Education, if a career counselor can learn about a client's traits that are relevant to work, he or she can help the client select employment best suited to them (2002). It soon becomes clear why trait-and-factor counseling has been described as matching people to jobs and criticized as the square-peg, square-hole theory.

Much of this approach came from Donald G. Paterson and later from E.G. Williamson. Williamson describes the counseling process as having six steps: analysis, synthesis, diagnosis, prognosis, counseling, and follow-up.

Ginzberg's Theories

Ginzberg's theories introduced the idea that starting at about age 18, individuals move from career exploration toward a series of events including educational specialization toward a specific career path and final commitment to a career. Ginzberg's stages include a fantasy stage, a tentative phase, and a realistic stage.

Super Developmental Framework

D.E. Super based his theory of career development on the idea that careers move through five distinct phases from childhood through adulthood. In addition, Super theorized that the choice of an occupation is highly influenced by each person's self-image and how this self-image mapped to people already in a particular occupation. The five phases, or stages, are

- *Growth stage*: As children, people develop a set of interests and values through their interactions at home, with neighbors, and in schools.

- *Exploratory stage*: From adolescence through the mid 20s, people's interests, aptitudes, and values solidify as they explore different roles and life situations.

- *Establishment stage*: By the mid 20s, people achieve, for the most part, stable careers.

- *Maintenance stage*: By 45, most people are settled into their occupations.

- *Decline stage*: Those retirees who are most successful carry over their work or vocational interests into retirement.

Personality or Typology

A number of theories exist that help explain the how and what of career choice. For example, career choice content theory centers its research on the consistency of career choices and how realistic these choices are in terms of how they match an individual's core strengths and characteristics. Another theory, **Roe's theory of occupation**, breaks occupations down into eight groups of service and six decision levels and is the basis for a number of tests to help determine best career choice based on interests. **Holland's occupational congruency model** seeks to match individuals to their best career choice through interviews that deal with six types of work environments: realistic (physical strength motor coordination, concrete problem solving), investigative (ideas and thoughts, intellectual activity), artistic (less personal interaction, self-expression), social (interaction with others), enterprising (use of verbal and social skills), and conventional (rules and regulations). **Psychodynamic theory** is also a tool to help predict career success, choice, and behavior by trying to understand what motivates individuals and the internal conflicts that exist in all human beings.

Behavioral Counseling

Behavioral career counseling is a scientifically precise approach to career decision making that leverages concepts from psychology. The approach notes that career-related behavior (such as job interview behavior) results from events in a person's past. Although complex in nature, career-related behavior can be broken down into its component parts. The client can then understand his or her own behavior. For example, a number of theories and models exist that help to explain career decision making. Krumboltz has provided a direct link between social learning theory and career development and decision making. **Krumboltz's**

model is known as the DECIDES model and is a rational decision-making process with seven steps:

1. Define the problem.

2. Establish an action plan.

3. Clarify values.

4. Identify alternatives.

5. Discover probable outcomes.

6. Eliminate alternatives systematically.

7. Start action.

Edgar Schein's Career Anchors Theory

The concept of *career anchors* was developed as a result of a 1961 study conducted by Edgar Schein at the Sloan School of Management at the Massachusetts Institute of Technology. The purpose of the study was to determine how careers in management developed and how well individuals faired with their employers. The study lasted 12 years and involved 44 alumni of the master's program. It was later expanded to include more than 200 people. One of the principal findings from the study was that as the individuals in the study learned more about themselves, their career choices were affected by this self-knowledge. If the individual moved away from this comfort zone, he or she was pulled back to the tenets of this self-knowledge and toward choices that suited him or her better. Schein categorized the basic drivers of these career decisions—talents, motives, and values—into eight career anchors that fit all individuals. The tool is used to help individuals gain personal insight and make choices.

Issues Associated With Career Planning Theories

Some common issues associated with the application of career planning theories include balancing the need for financial ROI with human capital and other organizational needs, working with and understanding the differences between generations and their approach to working in organizations, and the influence of cultural differences.

Human Capital and Organizational Need

The term *human capital* is commonly used in organizations and is generally defined as how individuals, corporations, and society develop some economic payback for investing in people. Organizations struggle with the task of showing this direct payback for investing in people and often the investments organizations make are based on the hope that the investment will pay off. Organizations increasingly ask for some direct evidence of this investment's bottom-line payback, which explains the growing popularity of evaluation methods, such as ROI, which is espoused by organizational expert Jack J. Phillips (2005). Although some HR functions do look at career planning in these terms, most still are reluctant to see employees in such stark dollars and cents terms.

Approaches to Work and Different Generations

New generations have different needs as they enter and leave the workforce. Baby boomers are just hitting their stride in terms of job position and income. Moreover, this generation is active into its fifties, unlike previous generations, and can look forward to 30 to 35 additional years of healthy and productive living. Baby boomers have also had great influence on the policy and procedures in organizations pushing for a more balanced work life.

Generation Xers and their values are the result of an era of two-income families, in which they grew up highly independent. They are self-reliant and do not mind being alone. In addition, generation Xers seek diversity, think in global terms, are technologically savvy, and value an informal atmosphere. The differences between these two generations should always figure into career development plans.

Multicultural Influences

Organizations are highly multicultural, and racial and cultural issues cannot be ignored in terms of career development. Bringing a diverse workforce together through a recognition and celebration of these differences is key and an important legal responsibility as well.

✓ Chapter 4 Knowledge Check

1. Which of the following best describes Williamson's trait and factor theory?

    a. Starting at the age of 18, people move from career exploration to a series of events including educational specialization toward a specific career path and a final commitment to a career.

    b. People can be understood in terms of the characteristics they possess such as intelligence, ambition, aptitude, and self-esteem.

    c. Careers move through five distinct phases from childhood through adulthood including growth, exploratory, establishment, maintenance, and decline stages.

    d. The consistency of career choices depends on a match between an individual's core strengths and characteristics.

2. Which of the following best describes Ginzberg's theory?

    a. Starting at the age of 18, people move from career exploration to a series of events including educational specialization toward a specific career path and a final commitment to a career.

    b. People can be understood in terms of the characteristics they possess such as intelligence, ambition, aptitude, and self-esteem.

    c. Careers move through five distinct phases from childhood through adulthood including growth, exploratory, establishment, maintenance, and decline stages.

    d. The consistency of career choices depends on a match between an individual's core strengths and characteristics.

3. Which of the following best describes the Super developmental framework?

    a. Starting at the age of 18, people move from career exploration to a series of events including educational specialization toward a specific career path and a final commitment to a career.

    b. People can be understood in terms of the characteristics they possess such as intelligence, ambition, aptitude, and self-esteem.

    c. Careers move through five distinct phases from childhood through adulthood including growth, exploratory, establishment, maintenance, and decline stages.

    d. The consistency of career choices depends on a match between an individual's core strengths and characteristics.

4. The personality or typology theories of career development help explain the how and what of career choice.

    a. True

    b. False

5. Who is credited with the DECIDES model, a seven-step, decision-making process that provides a direct link between social learning theory, career development, and decision making?

    a. Krumboltz

    b. Williamson

    c. Ginzberg

    d. Schein

6. Which of the following is not an issue associated with career planning theories?

    a. Human capital and organizational needs

    b. Approaches to work across different generations

    c. Multicultural influences

    d. Organizational structure

7. Occupational counseling is a scientific approach to career decision making that leverages concepts from psychology.

    a. True

    b. False

8. Roe's theory of occupation is a tool used to predict career success, choice, and behavior by trying to understand what motivates individuals.

    a. True

    b. False

References

Carter, R.T., ed. (2004). *Addressing Cultural Issues in Organizations.* London: Sage Publications.

Gray, C. (1998). *Enterprise and Culture.* London: Routledge.

Herriot, P., and R. Strickland, ed. (1997). "The Management of Careers." Special issue. *European Journal of Work and Organizational Psychology*, 5(4).

Leibowitz, Z.B. (1986). *Designing Career Development Systems.* San Francisco: Jossey-Bass.

Leiper, R. (2004). *The Psychodynamic Approach.* London: Sage Publications.

Millward, L. (2005). *Understanding Occupational & Organizational Psychology.* London: Sage Publications.

Osipow, S.H., and W.B. Walsh. (1988). *Career Decision Making.* Mahwah, NJ: Laurence Earlbaum Associates.

Phillips, J.J. (2005). *Investing in Your Company's Human Capital.* New York: AMACOM.

Stockdale, M.S., and F.J. Crosby. (2004). *Psychology and Management of Workplace Diversity.* United Kingdom: Blackwell.

Tunick, R.H. (2002). "Career Counseling: Traditional Approaches." West Virginia University white paper. Available at http://www.hre.wvu.edu/rtunick02/Career%20Counseling.htm.

Watts, A.G., et al (1996). *Rethinking Careers in Education and Guidance.* United Kingdom: Routledge.

Zemke, R. (2000). *Generations at Work.* New York: AMACOM.

5

Individual and Organizational Assessment Tools, Including Assessment Center Methodologies

The marketplace offers a variety of assessment tools that can facilitate the process of career planning and talent management by identifying individual strengths and improvement opportunities. These tools can also identify characteristics important for an organization's growth. In most situations, multiple assessments are used. The need for multiple assessments is related to the complexity of the construct being measured. For example, an assessment center approach may include a group exercise, a structured interview, a case study with written tasks, and a personality assessment. The key to using such assessment tools is to know the purpose of the tool, the validity and reliability of the evidence that supports it, and the inferences that are appropriately drawn from them. It also is important to know the weaknesses of a particular tool to avoid misuse.

Learning Objectives:

- ☑ List two types of multi-rater feedback tools and define each.
- ☑ Discuss the key differences between personality inventory instruments and personality tests.
- ☑ Identify the purpose and benefits of career profiles.
- ☑ Define the purpose of leadership assessments and list two types of leadership assessments.
- ☑ Summarize the issues associated with administering assessments, including validity, reliability, fairness, special accommodations, and legal issues surrounding testing.

Human Resource Audits

The *human resource audit* is one component of a succession planning system, building on the identification of successors and addressing the assessment of employee mobility to various positions. The audit identifies whether employees at various levels should stay in their current positions or if they should move to other positions and distinguishes key development strategies. It also helps designate pools of employees qualified for specific positions.

Each manager conducts a human resource audit by reviewing each direct report, including his or her

- time in current position

- performance

- readiness for advancement

- potential to move to a new position

- development required.

Having a plan in place ensures that all employees are reviewed whether they are potential future leaders or not, alleviating management's concern that succession planning is a selective program that ignores the development of certain employees.

If the system is linked to a staffing process, managers must then collect information on recommended next positions. A job-function code (such as sales, legal, human resources, and so forth) combined with salary information can help locate candidates for open positions in other parts of the organization. In this way, a person who is not a natural successor in his or her own unit could be considered in another part of the organization.

Figure 5-1 depicts a *succession summary* worksheet that can be used by the manager of a unit to choose successors.

Succession should be supported by performance appraisal programs or other means of providing viable, dependable employee skill information. With high-quality assessment information, managers can provide employees with effective development for future assignments. The following sections explore human resource assessments and audits.

Multi-Rater Feedback

Using multiple reviewers, or *multi-rater feedback*, is effective. In such a process, at least two levels of management review the employees and agree on their candidacy for specific positions. This evaluation process may be warranted under the following conditions:

- Manager judgments or experience levels are weak.

- There is a shortage of identified talent.

- The organizational culture supports structured programs.

Figure 5-1. Example of a Succession Summary Worksheet

Succession Summary

The position is listed first on the form because it is the focus of the planning process. Some optional pieces of data can be collected on the incumbents and replacements, such as Social Security or other employee identification numbers that are used in computer systems for retrieval of information. (International organizations often have employees who do not have Social Security numbers, so they would have to develop a numbering system.)

A job-function code identifies the type of job that an incumbent occupies or can fill in the future. This code is helpful if the system is expected to do candidate searches for similar positions. The probability of vacancy (PV) rating alerts the organization if a manager will be leaving in less than one year. The successor(s) are listed on the right of the form with their potential (PO), readiness (RE), and performance (PR) ratings.

Division: _____

Department: _____

Unit: _____

RATING MANAGER (Manager of Unit)	**JOB FUNCTION CODE** _____ SUCCESSION NAMES	**PV**	**PO**	**RE**	**PR**
POSITION:	(List candidates in order of preference.)				
NAME:	1. NAME:	___	___	___	___
ID#	ID#				
	2. NAME:	___	___	___	___
	ID#				
	3. NAME:	___	___	___	___
	ID#				

DIRECT REPORT POSITIONS	**JOB FUNCTION CODE** SUCCESSION NAMES	**PV**	**PO**	**RE**	**PR**
POSITION:	(List candidates in order of preference.)				
NAME:	1. NAME:	___	___	___	___
ID#	ID#				
	2. NAME:	___	___	___	___
	ID#				
	3. NAME:	___	___	___	___
	ID#				

NOTE: If you do not have an ID# for a person on the list, please contact your personnel or human resources representative for assistance.

PROBABILITY OF VACANCY
1. Within 12 months
2. Within 1-2 years
3. Beyond 2 years

POTENTIAL
1. Advance 2-3 levels
2. Advance at least 1 level
3. Move to a lateral position

READINESS
R. Ready now
F. Ready 1-3 years
Q. Promotability within 5 years is questionable
? Too early to evaluate

PERFORMANCE
1. Exceptional
2. Exceeds expectations
3. Meets expectations
4. Does not meet expectations
X. New in Position

JOB FUNCTION CODES
01 Finance/Accounting
02 Contracts Administration
03 Sales
04 Account Management
05 Public Relations & External Affairs
07 Human Resources
08 Security

09 Data Processing
10 Library
11 Purchasing
12 Material Handling & Distribution
13 Facilities & Plant Maintenance
14 Communications & Administrative Services
15 Executive Support & Planning & Business Development

16 Publications
17 Technical
18 Technical Support
20 Airplane Operations
21 Manufacturing Managers
23 General Managers & Executives
40 Legal

Source: Buckner and Slavenski (1993).

During the career planning process, assessments may be used in development planning. Two examples of multi-rater feedback instruments include 360-degree evaluations and assessment centers.

360-Degree Feedback

A *360-degree feedback* evaluation is a questionnaire that asks people—superiors, direct reports, peers, and internal and external customers—how well an employee performs in any number of behavioral areas. These raters should know the employee, and they should have opinions that the organization respects. Sometimes the employee also will want to rate himself or herself as a personal benchmark.

The rationale behind such a broad and well-rounded evaluation is simple: Upper management does not always see aspects of an employee's performance that others in the organization see.

This instrument is a questionnaire of statements, questions, or behaviors that users rate along an assigned scale (for example, "very satisfied" to "very dissatisfied"). These items are usually grouped together under category headings, and they usually discuss specific actions employees do or should do. Most instruments also include space for open-ended responses.

Assessment Centers

The term *assessment center* is a catch-all term that can consist of a variety of exercises. Assessment centers usually include oral exercises, counseling simulations, problem analysis exercises, interview simulations, role-play exercises, written report or analysis exercises, and group exercises. Assessment centers allow candidates to demonstrate more of their skills through job-relevant situations.

Assessment centers provide extremely accurate measures of performance and capability. Organizations using assessment centers have seen a high degree of predictability of employee success at more senior levels. These tools can be used for selection or development purposes, but the trend is more toward development.

Personality Type

When working with assessments, two terms are often used: personality inventory instruments and personality tests. What is the difference?

A *personality inventory instrument* provides an accurate picture of a person's personality type and indicates personality preferences. WLP professionals need to be adequately trained in their proper administration, scoring, and results interpretation for further planning.

A *personality test*, however, is usually a less formal and less accurate version. These tests can often be found on the Internet for generic, public use.

Many WLP professionals use personality inventory instruments because they address personality differences, information-processing styles, social interaction differences, and instructional preferences and can yield useful learner profiles. Two types of personality inventory instruments are the Myer-Briggs Type Indicator and the DiSC Personality Profile.

Myers-Briggs Type Indicator

The *Myers-Briggs Type Indicator (MBTI)* is one of the most widely used personality assessment instruments. Katherine Briggs and her daughter Isabelle Briggs Myers based their work on that of Swiss psychologist Carl Jung. The MBTI was *not* designed to assess level of maturity, degree of motivation, state of mental health, or level of intelligence.

DiSC

Based on the 1928 work of psychologist William Molton Marston, the *DiSC Personality Profile* uses a four-dimensional model in an assessment, inventory, and survey format. The results indicate dominance (direct and decisive), influence (optimistic and outgoing), supportiveness (sympathetic and cooperative), and conscientiousness (concerned and correct).

Career Profiles

A *career profile* is used in connection with a resume—a summary statement that highlights a person's work history and skills and competencies. This document is an excellent place to start to map a career path and to keep it on track. In an organization, it is a useful tool as a baseline record to map a path to a new position or career change.

Leadership Assessments

Leadership assessments identify developmental needs of current and future leaders at all levels in the organization. The assessment process helps organizations identify potential and helps employees develop career plans. These assessments may take several forms, including simulation-based or role-play-based assessments focusing on foundational, vital leadership skills such as decision making, delegating, gaining commitment, and coaching.

Issues to Consider When Administering Assessments

When developing and administering assessments, WLP practitioners should keep several considerations in mind, including validity, reliability, fairness, special accommodations, and legal issues.

Two terms a WLP practitioner may hear frequently in evaluation circles are *validity* and *reliability*. When reporting the results of an evaluation, a practitioner may be asked how he or she knows that the data is valid or the measures are reliable. Knowing these terms will help a practitioner respond intelligently. But more important, understanding these concepts can help practitioners construct better evaluation instruments such as questionnaires and tests.

Validity

Validity means measuring what the instrument was intended to measure. For example, if a group of e-learning participants misinterpret the intended meaning of a particular test question, the resulting data would not be valid. Verifying the validity of an evaluation instrument can involve complex statistics. Without the assistance of a statistician, the most practical way to improve the validity of evaluation instruments is to solicit feedback from SMEs. Practitioners should ask SMEs and participants to review each question with a critical eye. Practitioners should also administer the instrument to test subjects and compare their test results and perceptions of the questions' meanings with the intended meanings.

Reliability

Reliability refers to the ability to repeat the same measurement in the same way over time. Stated in a different way, reliability is concerned with the accuracy or precision of the instrument. Certain types of data are inherently reliable, such as a person's age. When evaluating this type of data, practitioners can feel confident that they will get reliable results every time. Other more subjective types of data can be much less reliable. Scientifically determining the reliability of an instrument requires that it be administered to a sample of subjects and undergo statistical analysis. Without scientific intervention, practitioners can still attempt to improve reliability by considering the types of data being measured and carefully wording questions to increase the likelihood that participants will respond consistently. Practitioners can also assess consistency by evaluating responses over time.

Fairness

If an assessment is to be used to qualify a person for a specific job, outside expertise often evaluates the test for **fairness**. The *Handbook of Psychological and Educational Assessment of Children* notes that fairness is a lack of bias, equitable treatment in the testing process, equality of outcomes of testing, and an equal opportunity to learn (Kamphaus and Reynolds 1990). The American Psychological Association offers a complete listing of fairness criteria that mirrors these basic principles.

Special Accommodations

When conducting assessments, WLP professionals must remember that civil rights legislation includes several implications to be considered for people with disabilities.

The most recent federal legislation to affect employers is the **Americans With Disabilities Act (ADA)** of 1990. This act prohibits discrimination in employment, public services, transportation, public accommodations, and telecommunications services against persons with disabilities.

Legal Issues Surrounding Testing

The employer bears the burden of proof to demonstrate that any given requirement for employment is related to job performance. The federal courts still evaluate any job requirement for job relatedness throughout the HR management and development cycle.

A potential legal problem for practitioners and their organizations occurs whenever a measure used for a significant employment decision, such as selection for a training program, is discriminatory. The question decided by federal courts is to what extent such a procedure has an "adverse impact on the hiring, promotion, or other employment or membership opportunities of members of any race, sex, or ethnic groups will be considered to be discriminatory…unless the procedure has been validated." (29 Code of Federal Regulations, Section 1607.3)

In the context of HRD, a decision to select someone for a training program is a test. For example, an interview to determine eligibility for a training opportunity is just as much a test under the law as the requirement to pass a pencil-and-paper assessment for verbal fluency for entry into an organizationally sponsored program.

Organizations may have an occasion to use testing in the training arena as a support for other organizational decisions. For example, the selection of employees may be based on criteria (posttest scores) generated from the training environment.

One legal question that needs to be addressed is to what extent pre-employment tests are based on successful completion of the program, or whether some other criterion, such as job performance, should be required by test developers.

✓ Chapter 5 Knowledge Check

1. Multi-rater feedback involves a process in which at least two levels of management review employees and agree on their candidacy for specific positions. Which of the following types of multi-rater feedback uses a questionnaire to ask superiors, direct reports, peers, and other internal and external customers how well an employee performs in a number of behavioral areas?

    a. Assessment centers

    b. Myers-Briggs Type Indicator

    c. Leadership assessments

    d. 360-degree feedback

2. Which of the following issues affects the development and administration of assessments and is concerned with the ability to repeat the same measurement in the same way over time?

    a. Reliability

    b. Validity

    c. Fairness

    d. Central tendency

3. The ADA guarantees an individual with a disability the right to a job for which he or she is applying.

    a. True

    b. False

4. Which of the following is best described as a component of succession planning that identifies whether employees should stay in current positions or move to other positions?

    a. Assessment centers

    b. Leadership assessments

    c. Multi-rater feedback

    d. Human resource audits

5. Assessment centers can contain a variety of exercises for employees to demonstrate skills through job-relevant situations.

    a. True

    b. False

6. Which of the following uses a four-dimensional model in an assessment, inventory, and survey format to indicate several characteristics, including dominance and optimism?

    a. Myers-Briggs Type Indicator

    b. DiSC Personality Profile

    c. Career profiles

    d. Leadership assessments

7. Which of the following is concerned with measuring what was intended to be measured?

    a. Fairness

    b. Reliability

    c. Validity

    d. DiSC

8. In the context of HRD, a decision to select someone to attend a training program is considered a test.

    a. True

    b. False

References

Buckner, M., and L. Slavenski. (1993). "Succession Planning." *Infoline* No. 259312.

Hastings, S. (2004). "Succession Planning: Take Two." *Infoline* No. 250405.

Kamphaus, R.W., and C.R. Reynolds, eds. (1990). *Handbook of Psychological and Educational Assessment of Children*. New York: Guilford Press.

Russell, S. (1997). "Training and Learning Styles." *Infoline* No. 258804.

Sample, J. (1993). "Legal Liability & HRD: Implications for Trainers." *Infoline* No. 259309. (Out of print.)

Shaver, W.J. (1995). "How to Build and Use a 360-Degree Feedback System." *Infoline* No. 259508.

Waagen, A. (1997). "Essentials for Evaluation." *Infoline* No. 259705.

6
Ethical Standards and Legal Issues in Career Counseling and Organizational Restructuring

 The career development and counseling professions have strict ethical standards regarding the confidentiality of employee information, especially as it relates to counseling and administration of psychological and personality tests. It is important to be aware of the various credentials that are required to administer the psychological and personality tests and to ensure that tests are being administered and results provided by certified professionals. It is important to understand the legal ramifications regarding career counseling as it relates to possible legal actions. It is also important to understand the impact of ethical standards as they relate to the use of information and guidelines for organizational restructuring.

Regulations of the *Equal Employment Opportunity Commission (EEOC)* govern the hiring, promotion, and discharge of employees. The regulations also cover training situations. The EEOC's Uniform Guidelines on Employee Selection Procedures "apply to tests and other selection procedures which are used as a basis for any employment decision...hiring, promotion, demotion.... Other selection decisions, such as selection for training or transfer, may be considered employment decisions if they lead to any of the decisions listed above."

This chapter explores some implications and aspects of and considerations about legal issues further.

Learning Objective:

☑ Identify and explain the credentials needed for a WLP professional to administer psychological and personality tests and guidelines around the retention and access of career counseling records.

Key Knowledge: EEOC and Civil Rights

EEOC: With regard to equal opportunity, this area of federal law is possibly the most unfamiliar to practitioners. The important legal issues for the human resources and training function involve lawful selection of individuals to participate in training and development programs. Practical examples of this issue are

- requiring training prior to job entry
- selecting employees to attend internal and external programs
- using tests in training as measures of job performance and retention
- making job assignments based on performance in the training program.

The employer bears the burden of proof to demonstrate that any given requirement for employment is related to job performance. The federal courts evaluate any job requirement for job relatedness throughout the human resource management and development cycle.

For regulatory requirements, many industries need employees to hold appropriate licenses and certifications. Training managers may be responsible for offering courses for licensing and certifications and maintaining a database that tracks all employees, their licensing status, and compliance with any ongoing training and licensing renewals.

Civil Rights: The Americans With Disabilities Act (ADA) of 1990 prohibits discrimination in employment, public services, transportation, public accommodations, and telecommunications services against people with disabilities. All aspects of employment are covered, including the application and selection process, on-the-job training, advancement in wages, benefits, and employer-sponsored social activities.

To be considered qualified for a position, a disabled job applicant or employee must be able to perform the essential functions of the job. Employers must reasonably accommodate known mental illness or physical disabilities unless they can demonstrate undue hardship. The ADA does not guarantee people with disabilities the right to a job to which they apply. Employers remain free to make decisions based on the skills or knowledge necessary for the job. An employer is not required to give preference to an applicant with a disability over an applicant without a disability.

With regard to the ADA and training implications, employers must ensure that employees with disabilities have reasonable accommodations that enable them to perform the essential functions of their jobs. Examples include offering auxiliary aids, such as interpreters, magnifying glasses to aid reading, taped text for those who are visually impaired, and instructional material with oversized lettering.

More information on legal issues and ethics is presented in Module 6, *Managing the Learning Function,* Chapter 15, "Legal, Regulatory, and Ethical Requirements."

7
Career Counseling Approaches

Career counseling is the direct application of the theories noted in Chapter 4. Experts in this area may be governed by state or professional counseling licensure or certifications from organizations such as state boards or professional associations. They also may come under legal or ethical standards, as established by state laws. Experts may choose from several theoretical models, often based on an individual employee's or client's background and needs. These practitioners use a variety of methods that best suit their clients, including personal assessments, web-based inventories and information, individual counseling, group or workshop formats, reading, and SMEs in the client's interest area. Experts assist the individual to identify vocational, avocational, and personal needs and to establish an IDP, or action plan, that they can use to achieve personal and professional success.

Learning Objectives:

- ☑ Summarize career counseling standards.
- ☑ List two prominent career counseling theories.
- ☑ Describe career counseling methods, including web-based options, vocational testing, and values-driven approaches.
- ☑ List and define three career development models.

Career Counseling Overview

Climbing the corporate ladder isn't as straightforward as it used to be. Individuals who were hoping to make a quick scramble to the top have to re-imagine their goals, rethink their strategies, and reevaluate what they think is important.

What should workers expect now? If they aren't guaranteed lifelong employment and automatic promotions, what will they get from their organizations—or for that matter, from work in general? The reverse question—What do organizations expect to get from their employees?—is also relevant.

As employees recognize these new rules and understand that they must manage their own career development, many do not know how to start. Others may begin a planning process but discover problems along the way and find no one there to help.

Even those employees who can discuss career issues with managers may face difficulties. Without support systems in place, employees may be reluctant to confide in managers.

Employees often are not the only ones who need help. Organizations need flexible employees who can respond quickly and efficiently to market demands and internal changes. To do this, organizations must anticipate and plan their employees' career needs. Development must be proactive, not reactive.

Organizations can help their employees—and ultimately themselves—answer these hard questions by implementing a career counseling system.

Before getting into the details of career counseling, it's necessary to understand some key terms and concepts in this area.

Career advising, a term often associated with educational institutions, is the professional guidance and recommendations employees can use to make good career decisions. ***Career advisors*** are the people responsible for this function.

Another clarification is the distinction between career guidance and career counseling. Table 7-1 outlines the key differences.

Some organizations hire career counselors, with master's degrees, as advisors or coaches. However, many career coaches are hired from the HR discipline. In general, any advisor should have good communication skills, knowledge of the organization, and a desire to help.

Key components of a generic career development process for employees include organized procedures to

- receive self-assessment and feedback
- gather organizational information about other departments, positions, competencies, trends, and company needs
- set goals and create development plans.

Table 7-1. Comparison of Career Guidance Versus Career Counseling

Career Guidance	Career Counseling
Is conducted by line managers and supervisors	Is conducted by trained career counselors
Occurs on a fairly regular basis. Once each year is typical	Occurs several times in a career
Focus is on • short- and long-term career objectives • performance-related strengths and weaknesses • relevant skills • relevant work experience • work-related training • company-related career interests	Focus is on • patterns of career satisfaction and dissatisfaction • broad-based occupational interests • work, personal, or interpersonal values • development of managerial, administrative, supervisory, and functional competencies
May or may not use a self-assessment process	Focuses on life priorities such as family issues, leisure activities or interests, and spiritual concerns
Goal is to match individuals to a particular job or career path	Goals are to teach a process and to provide direction

Career Counseling Standards

The National Career Development Association (NCDA) created 11 career counseling competencies. According to the NCDA, professional career counselors have a master's degree or higher and must demonstrate the knowledge and skills of a counselor with a career specialty. The 11 competency areas career counselors have proficiency in are career development theory, individual and group counseling skills, individual or group assessment, information and resources, program management and implementation, consultation, diverse populations, supervision, ethical and legal issues, research and evaluation, and technology. NCDA also has developed a series of ethical standards that career counselors should adhere to.

Career Counseling Theory

There are several theories to career development—which were noted in Chapter 4. They include Williamson's trait and factor theory; the Ginzberg and Super developmental frameworks; personality or typology theories, including Roe's theory, Holland's occupational congruency model, psychodynamic theory, and sociological theory; Krumboltz's behavioral theory; and Edgar Schein's career anchors theory. Career counselors have a deep understanding of these theories and translate them from theory into practice.

Career Counseling Methods

Career counseling can take several forms. With time pressures, privacy issues, and technology advancements, a new form of career counseling—often called career planning— has emerged online. The core issue facing web-based career counselors is the supposed inability to establish a core counselor-client relationship. To address this issue, as well as several others, the National Board for Certified Counselors approved a series of standards for counseling over the Internet in September 1997. Shortly after, the NCDA approved *Guidelines for the Use of the Internet for Provision of Career Information and Planning Services.*

Another tool career counselors use to help their clients is vocational testing. These tests help provide an idea of the kinds of careers that match a person's interests. One popular vocational test is the Strong-Campbell test. These types of tests also can help the counselor connect a client to a career that aligns with his or her core values. They support, clarify, and document impressions from an interview.

Finally, values-driven career counseling uses the individual's values to plan the direction he or she wishes to take. For example, if the person has a strong religious view, particularly in one specific faith, career counseling may advise seeking positions related to that particular faith. Another example might be a person who is seeking a job-sharing situation because he or she wants to have time at home for child or elder care.

Career Development Models

There are several models to consider when approaching career development. The traditional method is the climb-the-ladder, hierarchical approach to career advancement and development. This, just as is it sounds, is when a person seeks to move up the corporate ladder within an organization or an industry.

Another approach relates to the spiral career model. This is when someone develops skills in one industry and then moves on to a new area. This is often found among consultants and writers. Consultants have core consulting skills but may need to learn industry-specific skills, depending on their current client base. The same can be said for writers and journalists.

Other approaches to career development include attending workshops that provide relevant information and using self-assessment instruments. In addition, individuals can develop a career plan that outlines a method to reach a career goal, or conduct a career intervention— which is any activity that intends to further career development efforts.

✓ Chapter 7 Knowledge Check

1. All of the following are career counseling competencies except

   a. Research and evaluation

   b. Career development theory

   c. Individual or group assessment

   d. Adult learning theory

2. All of the following are examples of career development models except

   a. Spiral

   b. Hierarchical

   c. Self-assessment

   d. Career anchors

3. Career counseling is conducted by line managers and supervisors.

   a. True

   b. False

4. The primary goal of career guidance is to match an individual to a particular job or career path.

   a. True

   b. False

5. The primary issues facing web-based career counselors is/are

   a. Legal and ethical issues

   b. The use of vocational testing

   c. Maintaining confidentiality

   d. Establishing counselor-client relationships

References

Arthur, M.B., D.T. Hall, and B.S. Lawrence, eds. (1989). *Handbook of Career Theory.* United Kingdom: Cambridge University Press.

Leibowitz, Z.B., A.H. Souerwine, and J.E. McMahon. (1985). "Career Guidance Discussions." *Infoline* No. 258507.

Mitchell, L. (1996). *Peterson's The Ultimate Grad School Survival Guide.* Lawrenceville, NJ: Thompson Peterson's.

Mulcahy Boer, P. (2001). *Career Counseling Over the Internet: An Emerging Model for Trusting and Responding to Online Clients.* Mahwah, NJ: Lawrence Erlbaum Associates.

National Career Development Association. (1997). Career Counseling Competencies. Available at http://www.ncda.org/pdf/counselingcompetencies.pdf

Pope-Davis, D.B., et al. (2003). *Handbook of Multicultural Competencies.* United Kingdom: Sage Publications.

8
Coaching and Mentoring Approaches

 Coaching and mentoring are key programs that assist with career planning and talent management. A variety of approaches can be used to develop mentoring and coaching programs. The key to success with both programs is buy-in from top management as part of the organization's strategic initiatives. Coaching and mentoring programs are commonly used in organizations to identify high-potential employees and to assist in the growth and development of leaders. A development plan is critical in identifying learning objectives and outcomes for individuals who participate in these programs. The first step is to understand the difference between coaching and mentoring.

Learning Objectives:

- ☑ Describe the difference between coaching and mentoring.
- ☑ Explain how coaching and mentoring assist with career planning and talent management.

Key Knowledge: Coaching and Mentoring Approaches

Coaching is a continual process designed to help employees achieve greater competence and overcome barriers to improving competency once they have the knowledge or skills to perform job tasks. Coaching encourages people to do more than they ever imagined they could and is appropriate when the person has the ability and the knowledge to do the job but is not meeting performance expectations.

Coaching, in the narrowest sense, is the process of helping a single employee improve a particular aspect of his or her performance. In the broadest sense, it is the management role associated with high-performance teams. As such, it extends to training, facilitating, consensus building, conflict resolution, and boundary management. This set of skills and knowledge applies to the coach who deals with an individual learning on-the-job for the first time or trying to improve a weakness. They also apply to the coach who works with a team to improve performance and reach a new goal.

A coach's analytical skills are critical in determining the cause of a problem and in making a preliminary determination about what might be causing unsatisfactory performance. WLP professionals should keep in mind that not all performance issues can be solved through coaching—just as training can only solve performance gaps due to lack of knowledge or skill.

Coaching is an appropriate intervention if an employee does not understand the appropriate expectations, priorities, ways of correctly completing tasks, and the standards to which performance is measured. Coaching will not resolve performance issues due to performance obstacles such as a lack of resources, unrealistic expectations, or too many responsibilities unless the manager adjusts these external factors.

Peer coaching is also used frequently, particularly in team environments and especially within self-directed work teams.

It is ironic that in this time of technological achievement, the lifeblood of corporations is the accumulated insight of the people who choose to give their gifts of talent and commitment. So, the question is this: How do organizations ensure that the intellectual legacy of employees continues?

A large portion of the answer lies with ***mentoring*** initiatives. Mentoring is a powerful, dynamic process—for both employees and organizations. To share wisdom is to share life experience. No matter which method is used, mentoring has the potential to elevate corporate dialogue from the mundane to the truly transformational.

Coaching and Mentoring Approaches, continued

Mentoring is not for everyone, and a mentoring program will not solve all training needs. However, it is an ongoing process that provides an opportunity for a mentor to share skills; knowledge; and, most important, experience with a protégé. Mentoring differs from other types of supporting relationships often found in organizations, such as coaching. Coaching is more long-term and career-oriented; it requires understanding the context of the organization: politics, business, the power structure, and how to optimize it. Mentoring is more job or performance related. Mentoring is tactile whereas coaching is strategic. Mentoring is relationship-based learning in which the mentor and protégé work toward a common goal and both benefit from the experience.

A key benefit to mentoring programs is that they offer something other career development programs do not—individual attention. Traditionally, organizations have been interested in grooming employees to take over jobs of increasing responsibility. On another level, they might be concerned with retaining the bright, young graduates who are still testing the waters, but could easily take their skills and enthusiasm elsewhere if they are not quickly involved in the excitement, goals, and—most important—people of the organization.

Mentoring can take several forms, from an informal relationship in which a mentor helps a protégé learn a specific task to a long-term relationship in which a mentor provides advice and support to a protégé over a period of several years.

Formal mentoring focuses on long- or short-term goals based on the needs of the protégé and willingness and availability of the mentor and tends to focus on career development and overall career performance from a long-term perspective or over a period of time.

Structured mentoring is concerned with a protégé's acquisition of a particular skill set in the minimum amount of time. This type of mentoring is focused on specific behavioral objectives, clearly articulated expectations, and planned activities created for the purpose of providing the protégé with an opportunity to learn specific skills in a specific context.

More information on coaching and mentoring is presented in Module 7, *Coaching*, Chapter 3, "Coaching Competencies."

9

Performance Consulting Approaches

 Performance consulting pulls together techniques and tools from a variety of disciplines, including behavioral psychology, instructional design, organization development, and statistical analysis.

Performance consulting focuses on a systematic approach to identifying strengths and gaps that exist within an organization and within its human capital. Experts use a wide range of tools to identify systematic issues that affect organizational goals, including assessments and metrics that identify options, develop interventions, and measure results. They also help their clients establish goals linked to measurable outcomes and resolve performance gaps.

Practitioners employ cause-and-effect analysis tools to develop intervention strategies and evaluate results, and they balance systems issues with process issues. Ultimately, performance consultants ensure that individuals develop successful strategies.

In the beginning of all strategic performance improvement efforts is an assessment to systematically identify a specific individual, team, or organizational need. This assessment is performed through a series of analyses that identify the discrepancy between the actual versus desired performance, clarify the desired outcomes, set the boundaries of the issue to be addressed, and analyze all the factors that support and inhibit performance.

The goal is to determine what needs to be done and whether a difference has been made. The WLP professional needs to be able to ask the right questions about what is happening in the organization and to determine what the issue is that needs to be addressed. It is crucial at this stage to clarify the desired outcome required and to understand what is inhibiting the realization of this outcome. Root-cause analysis and solution design should flow out of this step.

Another key tenet of performance consulting and the human performance improvement (HPI) process is that training is not the solution to every performance issue—and is only appropriate when the performance gap is caused by a lack of knowledge or skill. Some other potential solutions include changes made to the work environment, processes, compensation and reward system, and so forth.

Learning Objective:

☑ Describe how performance consulting approaches, including tools and techniques from a variety of disciplines, assist with career planning and talent management.

Chapter 9

Key Knowledge: HPI Overview

HPI is based on the premise that there is a need for improvement or, more specifically, that there is dissimilarity between what is actually happening and an organization's desired state.

HPI is a comprehensive strategy that incorporates a set of methods or processes by which information is gathered. This information is used to develop interventions that provide effective, economical, and practical solutions to performance problems. Gap analysis is a critical activity carried out during the second stage of the HPI model—performance analysis.

The identification and definition of the performance gap is a crucial step in helping an organization address performance issues. Within the HPI model, the performance analysis has two distinct purposes:

- It identifies organizational performance goals and objectives.
- It gathers information about factors that influence performance.

The overall performance of an organization is measured by how well it meets the expectations of its customers. If the customer is not satisfied, the first question is "Why?" If the problem is unknown, it is difficult to find a solution. To find the right solution—one that will solve the problem, address the performance gap, and meet the customer's expectations—the practitioner must identify the discrepancy between actual and preferred performance levels. The goal is to discover and define the discrepancy.

The performance gap analysis should define the following factors: driving forces, restraining forces, current state, desired state, and methods for change.

The critical outcome of the gap analysis is the identification of the performance gap. This can be done using a single investigator or a group or team. The procedure used to gather information includes reviewing documents and records to learn about current performance levels as well as anticipated directions for the organization.

Various data-collection instruments and techniques—such as interviews, surveys, focus groups, and corrective action reports—may be used to gather the needed information. The choice of organizational research method depends on the size of the targeted performance group and the size of the group affected by the performer. The important goal to focus on is determining the performance that is the real issue.

HPI Overview, continued

The push for performance accountability is not a recent phenomenon. The HPI field has existed as a recognized area of study for decades. In short, increasing attention on performance is not a fad; it won't go away and will become more pervasive. Organizations and management are asking WLP professionals to be more accountable for performance results, and the training profession is moving toward a performance focus.

Why is the emphasis on performance and results increasing? The simple answer is that training can't solve most performance issues. Training addresses performance gaps caused by a lack of skill or knowledge, but training cannot improve motivation; change job designs, workflow, or organizational structure; or solve a host of other factors.

In short, a wide variety of research findings show that training isn't the solution to most performance gaps because the vast majority of poor performance is not due to poor skills or lack of knowledge—it's a result of other causes, such as process problems, motivation, incentive issues, resources, unclear standards, or confusing feedback. Uncovering the root of these individual problems and helping to solve them will go a long way in helping clients boost their marketability and therefore their career planning and talent management efforts. And, ultimately, it will go a long way to improving a company's bottom-line results.

More information on human performance improvement is presented in Module 3, *Improving Human Performance,* Chapter 2, "Business, Performance, and Gap Analysis."

10
Managerial and Leadership Development Best Practices

Managerial and leadership development is a deliberate effort to help individuals to perform effectively in their current positions by encouraging their capabilities. To be relevant, management development experts can plan and implement myriad strategic programs.

Learning Objectives:

☑ Explain the purpose of managerial and leadership development.

☑ List two formal and informal managerial and leadership development methods.

☑ Describe the characteristics of goal-oriented, activity-oriented, and learning-oriented learners and which types of programs might be best matched to each type.

☑ Explain how identified competency gaps can be addressed in managerial and leadership development programs.

Managerial and Leadership Development Overview

Almost any organization's mission statement is likely to refer to some value that the organization places on its employees. Organizations have long realized the benefit of developing their employees. However, not as many organizations have made developing management skills and performance a priority—likely because there is not a one-size-fits-all answer to implementing an appropriate development program. Or maybe it's because, until recently, organizations were not sure how to measure the effectiveness of the program, or if the program should be evaluated at all.

Management development does not differ from any other type of performance intervention. It consists of a systematic process to determine which components should be included in the program.

Patricia McLagan (1989) writes: "The demands on managers are changing. They must provide more leadership and less constraint, more anticipation and less reaction, more developed people and less developed activity, more cross-functional linkage and less functional individualism, more total enterprise decision making and less budget gamesmanship, more focus on outputs and less on activities."

With these changes in the roles of managers comes a need to develop programs that ensure managers have the skills required to make a positive impact on the goals and objectives of the organization. A strategic management and leadership development process enables companies to go the distance and increase their competitive knowledge.

The process for developing a new management development program (or revising an existing program) begins with analysis. It does not make sense to develop a program without first identifying what the organization expects of its managers and how well the managers currently meet those expectations.

Management development must be strategically linked to a company's business plan. For this reason, it should have its own budget line and not be an afterthought, as if there is an endless money supply. Solid links to business, human resource, and management development planning objectives give the management development process its strategic importance within the organization. Thus, the management development programs that are designed and implemented should reflect company goals and managerial needs.

Specific principles, objectives, and program components guide strategic management development. Although programs differ from one organization to another, three process principles remain constant:

1. Each manager is responsible for his or her own development.

2. Executives are responsible for the development of their subordinates.

3. The organization is responsible for providing opportunities for the growth of all managers.

This process encompasses managers at all levels, from the chief executive officer (CEO) to the front-line supervisors.

Management development recognizes the fluidity of a manager's role, the differences in roles among different managerial levels, and different competency levels that these roles require. The process demands that a company clearly delineate competencies and roles for managers at all levels.

A variety of program offerings strengthen management development. Too often organizations concentrate narrowly on formal training programs at the expense of equally effective programs, such as coaching, job rotations, performance appraisals, or committee and task-force assignments. The specific components of a management development program should address the specific performance needs of the organization and the specific needs of the managers.

The management development process ensures that the development and training a manager receives relates directly to his or her job duties and company goals. An evaluation strategy ensures that knowledge and skills gained through development programs relate well and easily transfer to the manager's job.

Formal and Informal Methods

Just as all other learning interventions may be formal or informal, the same is true for managerial and leadership development programs. Table 10-1 summarizes some formal and informal training programs.

Table 10-1. Formal and Informal Management Development

Formal	Informal
External education programs (for example, degree, certificate, or certification programs; executive master's of business administration)	Job-rotation programs
Internal group training programs	Position-assignment programs that expose individuals to various work duties, responsibilities, tasks, projects, or people
Succession planning programs	On-the-job coaching programs
Management or leadership career planning programs	Management or leadership mentoring or sponsorship
External group training programs (for example, programs offered by external vendors or university faculty)	Management and leadership self-study programs in which individuals initiate self-development learning projects
On-the-job training programs	Learning sabbaticals

Formal	Informal
	Management or leadership self-development (for example, independent efforts undertaken by adults to improve themselves and grapple with work-related and life-related challenges, which may include attending lectures, workshops, and conferences; taking self-assessments; and seeking out someone in another organization doing the same job to discuss concerns)

Types of Adult Learners and Seven Must-Follow Principles of Adult Learning

Adult learners are different from other learners. Motivation theorist Cyril Houle in his 1961 book *The Inquiring Mind,* identified three categories to explain the motivation of learners: goal-oriented learners, activity-oriented learners, and learning-oriented learners. Goal-oriented learners learn with a clear purpose in mind, such as career advancement. Activity-oriented learners' motivation for learning is the social interaction possibilities associated with learning. Learning-oriented learners want to learn because they have a predisposition for learning or learning for learning's sake.

When designing and developing management and leadership development programs, it is critical to remember these three categories of learners along with these seven key principles of adult learning:

1. **Adult learning is andragogy, not pedagogy.**

Andragogy, a term popularized by Malcolm Knowles (1988), refers to the art and science of teaching adults. Andragogy encompasses principles that instructional designers must address when preparing learning programs for adults. Pedagogy, on the other hand, refers to the art and science of teaching children, whose learning needs differ significantly from those of adults.

2. **Adult learners are pressed for time.**

Adults squeeze in learning between demanding jobs, family responsibilities, and community commitments. Even when highly motivated to learn, the call of life limits the time that many adults can invest in learning.

3. **Adult learners are goal oriented.**

Adults primarily participate in learning programs to achieve a particular goal. The goal may be work related, such as using a computer system more effectively or writing a performance plan that conforms to company guidelines. The learning goal might be personal, such as the desire to learn basic Japanese in advance of a vacation in Japan or learning Adobe Photoshop to prepare a family website. Classroom trainers often begin courses by asking learners how they hope to benefit from the course, and many trainers tailor their content accordingly.

4. Adult learners bring previous knowledge and experience.

Whenever possible, linking new material in a course to learners' existing knowledge and experience creates a powerful and relevant learning experience. In some instances, however, content in the training program contradicts material that people previously learned. In such situations, designers of training programs must first convince learners to part with the old approach so they can accept the new.

5. Adult learners have a finite interest in types of information.

Although many training courses tackle complex topics, most learners are primarily interested in aspects that directly affect them. In many cases, that's just a small part of the content.

In contrast, because they have so little time with learners, many trainers want to cram in as much content as they can. Because learners see limited application of the additional content, they absorb little of it, sometimes tuning out the content that directly affects them. In the classroom, instructors usually detect this situation when eyes glaze over with an "I'm overwhelmed" look.

6. Adult learners have different motivation levels.

During the first six weeks to three months on the job, adults are highly motivated to learn. When faced with a new work process or approach, adults are similarly motivated to learn. (What stifles their motivation, at this point, is fear of failure and difficulty of unlearning old habits.) As they become more familiar with the content, learners' motivation to learn wanes until a specific need arises. The challenge to designers of training programs is identifying the motivation level of learners as their expertise grows, and matching content to that level of motivation.

7. Adult learners have different learning styles.

Learning style describes an individual's approach to learning that involves the way he or she behaves, feels, and processes information. Each person has a number of preferred learning styles.

Need to Train to Meet Competency Gap

The goal of succession planning is to develop the next generation of leaders and managers by proactively determining competency gaps and then providing appropriate solutions to bridge the gaps in skills, knowledge, and competencies through various forms of informal and formal learning.

The management development process has a broad yet business-driven orientation. This process prepares managers—no matter which slot they occupy on the organization chart— to manage better, bridge the gaps, and achieve company business objectives.

These are several principles that underlie the management development process and guide its implementation:

- *Culture and management style:* The company's culture and management style are well known to all employees. A model exists for management knowledge and skills, and the management-development process supports this model.

- *Responsibility for development:* Managers have the primary responsibility for their own development. However, the organization provides development and training opportunities and encourages managers to engage in self-development activities.

- *Linkage to business strategy:* Management development is linked closely to business strategy. For each business objective, management development needs are clarified, timetables are set, and resources are allocated.

- *Top management support:* Top management gives support to the management development process. Executives support the program, take part in needs assessment activities, and avail themselves of development opportunities. They begin by making sure that management development strategies link to business objectives.

- *Program design:* Management development programs are designed and updated according to the needs, strengths, and learning styles of managers in the organization. Programs are cost-effective and based on direct application to managerial duties or development.

- *Process:* The management development profession focuses on results and impacts and is an integral part of the HRD system.

- *Media to support the process:* Various media, including online learning technologies and collaboration tools, support and facilitate management and leadership development programs.

✓ Chapter 10 Knowledge Check

1. Which of the following is an example of an informal leadership development method?

   a. Succession planning programs

   b. Job rotations

   c. On-the-job training

   d. Management and leadership self-study

2. Which of the following best describes the purpose of managerial leadership and development?

   a. To affect organizational goals and objectives

   b. To provide guidance and coaching to employees

   c. To create individual development plans for workforce planning

   d. To direct the work of individuals in a department

3. All of the following are principles to guide strategic management development except

   a. Each manager is responsible for his or her own development.

   b. Executives are responsible for the development of their subordinates.

   c. The organization is responsible for providing opportunities for the growth of all managers.

   d. Subordinates are responsible for their own self-initiated learning and career development.

4. In any organization, the following three principles hold true: each manager is responsible for his or her own development, executives are responsible for the development of their subordinates, and the organization is responsible for providing opportunities for the growth of all managers.

   a. True

   b. False

5. The managerial development process recognizes the fluidity of a manager's role, the differences in roles among different managerial levels, and different competency levels that these roles require.

   a. True

   b. False

6. The management development process is different from any other learning intervention.

   a. True

   b. False

References

Carliner, S. (2003). *Trainer Design Basics*. Alexandria, VA: ASTD Press.

Jarvis, P., J. Holford, and C. Griffin. (2003) *The Theory and Practice of Learning*. Oxford, United Kingdom: Routledge Taylor and Francis and Group.

Knowles, M. (1988). *The Modern Practice of Adult Education: From Pedagogy to Andragogy*. Cambridge, MA. Cambridge Book Company.

McLagan, P. (1989). *Models for HRD Practice*. Alexandria, VA: ASTD. (Out of print.)

Piskurich, G. (2003). *Trainer Basics*. Alexandria, VA: ASTD Press.

Russell, S. (1987). "The Management Development Process." *Infoline* No. 258711.

11
Performance Management Systems and Techniques

 Performance management systems provide a methodology and tools to translate organizational goals and outcomes into individual employee job expectations and to define the competencies or skills needed to carry them out. This includes establishing a process to create guidelines for supervisors and to set expectations, coach, and assess individual employee achievements. Organizations use performance management systems to measure individual contributions to the organization and also link the system with other HR systems, such as compensation and talent management. Because they relate to other HR functions, such systems must stand the test of legal defensibility against such standards as the federal EEOC Uniform Guidelines on Employee Selection Procedures. Organizations also use performance management systems to track employee development, including acquisition of new or higher levels of competencies, skills, or knowledge. Success of such systems often is dependent on the relationship between the supervisor and employee, and the communication and feedback about to the individual's performance toward the achievement of defined goals.

Learning Objective:

☑ Explain how other HR functions, such as employee relations, job analysis, and defining and communicating evaluation methodologies are crucial to career planning and talent management processes in an organization.

Key Knowledge: Performance Management

Planning for career development in an organization doesn't happen in a vacuum. Career development is a core component of HRD that integrates with several other HR functions, including selection, compensation, performance management, and job design.

Recruitment and selection: Building organizational capacity means developing a talented workforce to meet business and customer needs. For many organizations, attracting and retaining the right talent is their primary business need. How can career development and training help with recruitment and selection? A 1999 Kepner-Tregoe report found that the top three reasons employees left their organizations were perceived lacks of financial rewards, recognition, and career development. The bottom line: If employees don't receive training and career development at their current workplaces, they will go elsewhere.

Compensation: Training managers should look at compensation not as a way to drive performance, but as a message to employees about what results their organizations value. Four links need to connect performance and rewards: measurement of valuable results, accomplishment of results, accomplished results being rewarded, and rewarded results being valued. Many organizations switch to variable pay options as a way of updating compensation practices.

Performance management: Performance management has often been described as the process of developing, motivating, deploying, and aligning people to increase business performance. To aid in this process, HR uses computer-based performance management systems to understand which employees need to develop required skills and expertise.

Job design: J.R. Hackman and G.R. Oldham's (1975) job characteristics model explains in detail how to make jobs more interesting and motivating for employees. In this model, every job has five characteristics that determine how motivating workers will find it. These characteristics determine how employees react to their jobs and lead to outcomes such as high performance and satisfaction and low absenteeism and turnover. The characteristics are skill variety, task identity, task significance, autonomy, and feedback.

Hackman and Oldham argue that these five characteristics influence an employee's motivation because they affect three critical psychological states. If employees believe their work is meaningful and that they are responsible for outcomes and for knowing how those outcomes affect others, they will find the work more motivating; be more satisfied; and, therefore, perform at a high level.

More information on performance management is presented in Module 6, *Managing the Learning Function,* Chapter 12, "HR Systems."

12

Approaches to Maximize Workplace Diversity

A variety of approaches are used to maximize workplace diversity. Organizations use diversity initiatives to reflect the changing population of the general workforce. It is important that there is an awareness of the various aspects of diversity and appropriate methods are used to meet strategic initiatives for a diverse population. These initiatives should not only focus on race, ethnicity, and gender, but should also include generational concerns.

Instruments are available to assess workforce diversity. It is important that diversity programs provide an awareness of diverse groups and global populations. This growing trend needs to be taken into consideration in career planning and talent management programs.

Organizations invest in diversity programs for a variety of reasons, with the changing demographics of the workforce being the most compelling. The Hudson Institute issued a striking forecast describing these changes, commonly known as the Workforce 2000 report. The institute's research suggests that women, immigrants, and minorities currently make up—and will continue to make up—a growing portion of new entries into the workforce. This literally changes the face and needs of the workforce and the consumer market.

Organizations that rely on their workforces to help them with productivity, quality, flexibility, and innovation must understand what motivates employees. What used to work does not always work now. In addition, more businesses are competing in a global market. This economic focus requires skills in cross-cultural communication and necessitates valuing different cultural models.

Learning Objectives:

- ☑ Compare and contrast high-context and low-context cultures and discuss how communication differs when dealing with each of these.
- ☑ Explain considerations regarding personal space and workplace diversity training.
- ☑ List two strategies that are used to create diverse workforces.
- ☑ Provide two examples of the needs of the baby boomer generation versus generation X employees and how this may have an impact on developing career planning programs.
- ☑ Identify strategies that could be used to facilitate inclusion in multi-racial, multi-generational environments.

Cultural Awareness

According to Kieran McBrien, author of *Developing Localization Friendly E-Learning* (2005), if a training professional is developing e-learning or classroom training that will be used globally, he or she needs to plan for cultural portability.

Culture involves the way people look at the world—a shared value system. It includes language and many other things as well, such as the value a society puts on individualism or group action, tolerance for uncertainty, willingness to take risks, the comfort level in interacting with a teacher and peers, and so forth. These and other factors have a direct effect on learning styles and how people interact on the job.

In countries such as the United States, Canada, and Australia, learners are used to getting to the point quickly, whereas many Europeans expect a more structured approach. Asians may prefer to master theory before digging into facts.

For managerial and leadership programs, training materials should ideally be entirely different for each country or culture. The programs should take into account all issues of language, world view, learning style, and content. However, this is rarely feasible. Instead, training materials and other software applications need to be designed from the start with multilingual and multicultural participants in mind.

According to Rhinesmith (1996), there is a major cultural influence on training outside the United States. This was explored by Geert Hofstede, who identified a range of variables that also affect instructional design in different world cultures.

One of his dimensions is power distance, or the degree to which a society places emphasis on differences in status and authority relationships. Table 12-1 outlines some of the variables affected by power distance differences.

Table 12-1. Power Distance Differences

High Power Distance	Low Power Distance
Formal relationships	Informal relationships
High dependence	Low dependence
Teacher oriented	Learner oriented
Highly personal	Impersonal
Status emphasis	Equality emphasis
Fixed approach	Variable approach
Conformity	Experimentation

Source: Rhinesmith (1996).

In high-power-distance cultures, more traditional teacher-student relations are emphasized. In such a situation, one major factor to be contended with is student initiative. Students expect the teacher to take the initiative, and it is not natural for students to volunteer their opinions or participate in classroom discussions without being explicitly called upon.

For example, one trainer conducted a seminar in Japan and spoke for 13 hours straight over two days without a question. He had been told in advance that this was the way the participants would prefer to operate, and that participants would ask questions at the end of the session after small groups had a chance to discuss the ideas presented in the seminar.

These culture concepts and differences need to be considered when designing and delivering managerial and leadership programs.

Gender and Race Awareness

Years after the Civil Rights Act of 1964, American corporations still struggle with discrimination in the workplace. State and federal equal opportunity agencies receive and process thousands of discrimination claims each year, and the price tag associated with these complaints has skyrocketed. In recent years, many highly publicized racial and sex discrimination lawsuits and settlements have forced organizations to devote more attention to better management of stereotyping through more effective diversity training.

Many of these organizations have instituted programs that have made them role models in diversity training. Although preventing lawsuits may be a good reason for embracing more extensive diversity measures, many organizations are realizing that such activities are also good for the bottom line.

Generational Differences

A lack of understanding of how different generations perceive and approach things can often lead to strong conflicts. The book *Global Leadership: The Next Generation* succinctly and aptly explains work in a multigenerational environment: "What we mean by multigenerational is leading individuals with different frames of reference or ideological differences. The history, politics, and economic environment in which an individual is raised will strongly impact his or her skills, abilities, and perspectives in all situations. For instance, in the United States, those born in the baby boomer generation grew up with the Vietnam War and Watergate. As a result, there is a lack of trust in government. On the other hand, the generation before them grew up in a time of war heroes and a post-Depression economic environment. These environmental differences will impact generational views of a business" (Goldsmith, et al. 2003).

Personal Space

The way individuals use space varies greatly from culture to culture and is often steeped with cultural associations. Germans, for example, generally use space to reinforce social distance. This increased social distance may appear cold and isolating by U.S. standards.

Whereas a German manager may place emphasis on the physical separation of his or her office, a Japanese manager usually has no separate office. Instead, status is indicated by the position of his or her desk in a large open area filled with other desks. The manager's desk is usually farthest from the door, near a window, and placed so that the entire work area is visible. Danger lies in the possibility that a German or American entering a Japanese environment might misread the Japanese seating arrangement as egalitarian.

Proxemics is the relationship of people's positions in space. Anthropologist Edward T. Hall defined four spatial relationships among adults in the United States:

- *intimate:* 18 inches around the body, for family and lovers
- *personal:* 18 inches to four feet, for family and friends
- *social:* four to 12 feet, for co-workers and social acquaintances
- *public:* More than 12 feet, for platform speakers and entertainers.

As Hall and others have explained, when a person believes someone is too close, he or she feels threatened; however, people don't like the company of someone they find standoffish either.

People from the United States may encounter difficulties in communicating with people from other cultures because of this distance issue. The U.S. arm's-length approach may be uncomfortable in societies where friendly or serious conversations are conducted close enough to feel the other's breath on one's face.

Studies of workplace proxemics have shown that a business leader may select a participatory round table or may choose to head meetings from the end of a rectangular table. When given a choice, friendly co-workers tend to sit beside each other at a table, and mere acquaintances or enemies in office politics tend to sit opposite one another.

Disability Awareness

Civil rights legislation has several implications to be considered during training design, including participants with disabilities and multiple languages.

The most recent federal legislation to affect employers is the American With Disabilities ACT (ADA) of 1990. This act prohibits discrimination in employment, public services, transportation, public accommodations, and telecommunications services against persons with disabilities.

All aspects of employment are covered, including the application process and selection, on-the-job training, advancement in wages, benefits, and employer-sponsored social activities.

To be considered a qualified person with a disability, the job applicant or employee must be able to perform the essential functions of the job. Employers must reasonably accommodate known mental illness or physical disabilities unless undue hardship can be demonstrated.

The ADA does not guarantee an individual with a disability the right to a job for which he or she is applying. The employer remains free to make decisions based on the particular skills or knowledge necessary for the job. An employer is not required to give preference to an applicant with a disability over another applicant without a disability.

With regard to the ADA and training implications, employers must provide employees with disabilities with reasonable accommodations to enable them to perform the essential functions of the job. Examples include offering auxiliary aids such as interpreters, magnifying glasses to aid reading, taped text for those who are visually impaired, and instructional material with oversized lettering. These aids should be considered when designing both instructor-led training and e-learning.

Training Implications for Multiple Languages

For both classroom-based training and e-learning, intercultural communication and multiple languages can cause several barriers to training transfer. For instructor-led and classroom training, training managers may need to provide instruction and training materials in multiple languages to aid in learning transfer. These are some considerations:

- *Accent and linguistics:* An accent is the way an individual pronounces, enumerates, and articulates words. Trainers and managers need to consider the trainer and participants and try to provide an instructor who speaks the same language and has a similar accent or dialect as the participants.

- *Gross translation errors:* When translating training materials into multiple languages, gross translation errors are relatively frequent and usually are the easiest to detect and correct. Many errors are simply ridiculous or silly. The General Motors slogan "Body by Fisher," for example, was once translated into "Corpse by Fisher." The possibility of conflict arises when one party attributes the mistranslation as disrespect for the receiving culture.

- *Nuance errors:* When two parties do not have similar command of a language, mild distinctions between meanings can lead to misunderstandings. The nuances between misunderstand and misinterpret, for example, comments on the ability of an individual to understand.

Inclusion Approaches

WLP practitioners may identify the need to facilitate inclusion of new cultural ideas or minority and gender groups during training analysis and planning processes for management development programs. During this process, the HRD function and top management may develop a strategy to interview and hire for differences to broaden diversity within the organization.

To help facilitate inclusion of employees within the organization while minimizing differences, many organizations celebrate differences to help build awareness of different cultures and groups.

Organizations also may emphasize that differences combine to create unique opportunities, using the whole is worth more than the sum of its parts rationale.

Many organizations may try to become high-performance organizations that try to embrace and encourage diversity as well.

Several approaches used to facilitate inclusion are

- awareness
- modeling
- targeted interventions
- desensitization
- training.

✓ Chapter 12 Knowledge Check

1. High-power-distance relationships are learner-oriented.

    a. True

    b. False

2. Which of the following space guidelines between adults is most appropriate for co-workers and social acquaintances (in the United States)?

    a. 18 inches

    b. 18 inches to four feet

    c. Four to 12 feet

    d. 12 or more feet

3. Proxemics refers to

    a. Gender awareness

    b. Personal space

    c. Facilities planning

    d. Arrangement of seating in a U-shape

4. All of the following are strategies to create a diverse workforce except

    a. Modeling

    b. Targeted interventions

    c. Training

    d. Evaluation

5. The history and economic and political factors of a generation have no influence on the skills and abilities of those adults to learn.

    a. True

    b. False

6. Which of the following refers to a situation in which two individuals do not have a similar command of a language and may experience a misunderstanding because of mild distinctions between meanings of words?

    a. Accent and linguistics

    b. Gross translation errors

    c. Proxemics

    d. Nuance errors

References

Finkel, C., and A.D. Finkel. (2000). "Facilities Planning." *Infoline* No. 258504.

Finn, T. (1999). "Valuing and Managing Diversity." *Infoline* No. 259305.

Goldsmith, M., et al. (2003). *Global Leadership: The Next Generation.* Upper Saddle River, NJ: Pearson Education.

Hall, E.T. (1969). *The Hidden Dimension.* Garden City, NJ: McGraw-Hill.

Marquardt, M. (1999). "Successful Global Training." *Infoline* No. 259913.

McBrien, K. (May 2005). "Developing Localization Friendly E-Learning." *Learning Circuits.* Available at http://www.learningcircuits.org/2005/may2005/mcbrien.htm.

Rhinesmith, S. (1996). "Training for Global Operations." In R.L. Craig, ed., *The ASTD Training and Development Handbook.* 4th edition. New York: McGraw-Hill.

Sheftel, P.A., and M. Bennett. (2001). "How to Resolve Conflict." *Infoline* No. 250104.

13

Resources for Career Exploration and Lifelong Learning

Employees of all ranks and careers, as well as WLP professionals, should continuously explore their career and pursuit of lifelong learning to ensure career continuity and proliferation. As experts in this area, practitioners should be aware of the trends and changes in the workplace and be familiar with various resources.

Learning Objectives:

☑ Discuss the purpose of career exploration and lifelong learning and the types of resources that can be used during this process.

☑ Discuss how IDPs, informational interviews, and job rotations support career exploration and lifelong learning.

Human Capital

Building a successful career has never been more demanding. Globalization, social and political upheaval, rapid shifts in markets and business priorities, the use of outsourcing as a competitive tool, and the loss of the traditional employee-employer contracts have conspired to make building a career inside most organizations difficult. WLP professionals (as well as human resource and information technology professionals) are uniquely positioned to experience the fallout from these challenges. With few exceptions, professionals face

- increasing levels of accountability

- increasing levels of competition

- increasing responsibilities and top-down expectations

- increased exposure to positioning, posturing, and politics

- decreasing job security and longevity.

These tough realities mean that people must continually work to develop professionally and must sharpen their organizational survival skills as part of a lifelong learning commitment.

What's In It for Me? (WIIFM)

Many instructional programs are designed to introduce the WIIFM concept to orient users to the key benefits of the program and to help motivate them to learn.

Before developing career and organizational success skills, people need to think about their careers and lives within the organization. They should ask themselves, "What do I really need to know or do to succeed here?" The answers will depend very much on their personal goals and attitude toward lifelong learning. Definitions of thriving or succeeding in an organization may include

- being challenged

- seeing the bigger picture and contributing to the effort

- experiencing job satisfaction

- receiving good performance reviews and raises

- getting increased responsibility and authority

- supervising others

- advancing in the organization.

Each person defines success differently, just as responsibilities and promotions vary depending on the desired outcomes.

The WIIFM mentality also applies in the realm of taking charge of and managing a career. To set the right course, a person must know where he or she wants to go. Practitioners assisting people in developing their careers should consider the following questions:

- Is the work fulfilling and challenging?

- Does the person understand how he or she fits into the organization's strategy and goals?

- Is there a position in the organization to which he or she aspires?

- Does the person feel as though he or she has significant knowledge and talents that are untapped?

- Does he or she have balance in his or her life? Or does the person experience a significant amount of stress?

- Is there a different job that the person would like to try?

- Does he or she feel that he or she has sufficient opportunities to learn and expand skills?

The importance of these questions bears different weight depending on the individual and his or her commitment to lifelong learning. For some, having a sense of job satisfaction may be more important than advancing in the organization and vice versa.

IDPs (Individual Development Plans)

IDPs identify areas that an employee needs to develop currently and in the future as part of a lifelong learning philosophy; several notable companies have systems in place that make it easy for employees to fulfill development needs. An effective IDP not only benefits the individual employee, but it also helps the organization by narrowing performance and skills gaps.

But how are IDPs created? According to William J. Rothwell (2001), author of *Effective Succession Planning,* "An individual development plan (IDP) results from a comparison of individual strengths and weaknesses on the current job and individual potential for advancement to possible key positions in the future. Preparing an IDP is a process of planning activities that will narrow the gap between what individuals can already do and what they should do to meet future work or competency requirements in one or more key positions."

Informational Interviews

Informational interviews can serve as an enormous resource for someone going through the career-exploration process. They are an excellent way to gain invaluable knowledge about a particular career field or industry. Although they are not job interviews per se, informational interviews can help someone make industry contacts. Unlike a job interview, in an informational interview, the person seeking a career change asks the questions. The answers to these questions will help provide important career-choice information.

Job Rotation

Job rotations provide an employee with the opportunity to work in a new position, develop cross-functional skills, and determine if the role is a position that he or she would like to advance to permanently in the future. There are several types of job rotations. These are a couple of examples:

- *Cross-functional job rotations:* This is a formal program of temporary job rotations in which managers and employees take on new responsibilities.

- *Cross-country job rotations:* This is also a formal program for international organizations in which managers or other employees are assigned to a company department in another country.

The benefit for the organization is a better-rounded workforce with knowledge in cross-functional areas and the ability to determine which employees are a best fit for other roles within the succession planning process.

Multiple Modalities for Learning

To help someone learn new skills to help advance his or her career, WLP professionals can introduce one of the many learning interventions that can help individuals bridge skill gaps. Online learning enables individuals to access anytime, anywhere learning and information. Workshops and other types of facilitative or instructor-led training help improve psychomotor and cognitive skills and knowledge, which might be difficult to gain via a web-based delivery medium.

✓ Chapter 13 Knowledge Check

1. All of the following are examples of resources used in career exploration except

    a. IDPs

    b. Informational interviews

    c. Job rotation

    d. Personality type indicators

2. A cross-functional job rotation is a formal program for international organizations in which managers or other employees are often assigned to a company department in another country.

    a. True

    b. False

3. Which of the following results from a comparison of individual strengths and weaknesses on the current job and individual potential for advancement to key positions in the future?

    a. IDPs

    b. Informational interviews

    c. Job rotation

    d. Personality type indicators

4. Informational interviews are similar to job interviews in that a candidate applies for a particular job.

    a. True

    b. False

References

Pietrzak, T. (2005). "Building Career Success Skills." *Infoline* No. 250501.

Rosen, S., and C. Paul. (1997). "Career Renewal." San Diego, CA: Academic Press.

Rothwell, W.J. (2001). *Effective Succession Planning.* 2nd edition. New York: AMACOM.

Russell, Susan. (1987). "The Management Development Process." *Infoline* No. 258711.

Appendix A
Glossary

360-Degree Feedback Evaluation is a questionnaire that asks people—superiors, direct reports, peers, and internal and external customers—how well a manager performs in any number of behavioral areas.

ADA (Americans With Disabilities Act) is an act passed in 1990 that prohibits discrimination in employment, public services, transportation, public accommodations, and telecommunications services against persons with disabilities.

Andragogy (from the Greek meaning "adult learning"), the adult learning theory popularized by Malcolm Knowles, is based on five key principles that influence how adults learn: self-concept, prior experience, readiness to learn, orientation to learning, and motivation to learn.

Assessment Center is a catch-all term that includes a variety of exercises, including oral exercises, counseling simulations, problem analysis exercises, interview simulations, role-play exercises, written report or analysis exercises, and group exercises.

Audience Analysis is an analysis that is conducted to understand the target population, demographics, and other relevant information prior to job analysis, training, or other intervention.

Behavioral Career Counseling is a scientifically precise approach to career decision-making that leverages concepts from psychology.

Career Advising is the professional guidance and recommendations employees can use to make good career decisions.

Career Advisors, also called organizational career coaches, are the people responsible for career advising.

Career Profile is a summary statement that highlights a person's work history and skills and competencies.

Coaching is a process in which a more experienced person, or coach, provides a worker or workers with constructive advice and feedback with the goal of improving performance. (See also *Mentoring*, which focuses on career development and advancement.)

Cost-Benefit Analysis is a type of ROI analysis used to prove that an intervention either paid for itself or generated more financial benefit than costs.

DiSC Personality Profile uses a four-dimensional model in an assessment, inventory, and survey format, based on the work of William Molton Marston.

Edgar Schein's Career Anchors Theory is a concept developed as a result of a 1961 study by Edgar Schein conducted at the Sloan School of Management at the Massachusetts

Institute of Technology. The purpose of the study was to determine how careers in management developed and how well individuals faired with their employers.

Environmental Analysis helps establish a strategic plan for HRD programs and helps practitioners determine organizational strengths and weaknesses (internal) and opportunities and threats (external).

EEOC (Equal Employment Opportunity Commission) regulations govern the hiring, promotion, and discharge of employees, as well as training situations.

Fairness is a lack of bias, equitable treatment in the testing process, equality of outcomes of testing, and an equal opportunity to learn.

Ginzberg's Theories pushed the idea that starting at the age of 18 individuals move from career exploration toward a series of events including educational specialization toward a specific career path and a final commitment to a career.

Holland's Occupational Congruency Model seeks to match individuals to their best career choice through interviews that deal with six types of work environments: realistic (physical strength, motor coordination, concrete problem solving), investigative (ideas and thoughts, intellectual activity), artistic (less personal interaction, self-expression), social (interaction with others), enterprising (use of verbal and social skills), and conventional (rules and regulations). (See also *Occupational Congruency Model*.)

HRD (Human Resource Development) is the term coined by Leonard Nadler to describe the organized learning experiences of training, education, and development offered by employers within a specific timeframe to improve employee performance or personal growth. Also, it is another name for the field and profession sometimes called training or training and development.

Human Capital is a term used to describe the collective knowledge, skills, competencies, and value of the people in an organization.

Human Resource Audit is one component of a succession planning system, building on the identification of successors and addressing the assessment of employee mobility to various positions.

IDPs (Individual Development Plans) are plans for improvement in a current job or job advancement. These plans may or may not be tied to a performance appraisal system; however, a good plan usually is integrated with a performance appraisal.

Job Descriptions generally explain the duties of a job, but do not get into the specific tasks that a job performer must do to fulfill the stated duties.

Job Functions are major responsibilities of programs or departments that have specific outputs and outcomes for internal and external clients.

KSA is an abbreviation that has two definitions: **1.** Knowledge (or cognitive), skills (or psychomotor), and *attitude* (or affective) are the three objective domains of learning defined by Benjamin Bloom's taxonomy in the 1950s. **2.** Knowledge, skills, and *ability* are commonly referred to as KSAs and are used by federal and private hiring agencies to determine the attributes or qualities that an employee possesses for a particular job.

Krumboltz's Model is known as the DECIDES model and is a rational decision-making process with seven steps: **1.** Define the problem. **2.** Establish an action plan. **3.** Clarify values. **4.** Identify alternatives. **5.** Discover probable outcomes. **6.** Eliminate alternatives systematically. **7.** Start action.

Leadership Assessments identify developmental needs of current and future leaders at all levels in the organization.

Learning Style describes an individual's approach to learning that involves the way he or she behaves, feels, and processes information.

Mentoring is the career development practice of using a more experienced individual tutor or group to share wisdom and expertise with a protégé over a specific period of time. There are three types of mentoring commonly used: one-on-one, group, or virtual.

Multi-Rater Feedback is a process in which at least two levels of management review the employees and agree on their candidacy for specific positions.

Myers-Briggs Type Indicator (MBTI) consists of categories that identify 16 types of personalities based on extraversion or introversion, intuiting or sensing, thinking or feeling, and judging or perceiving. It is used in career development and team building.

Occupational Congruency Model seeks to match individuals to their best career choice through interviews that deal with six types of work environments: realistic (physical strength motor coordination, concrete problem solving), investigative (ideas and thoughts, intellectual activity), artistic (less personal interaction, self-expression), social (interaction with others), enterprising (use of verbal and social skills), and conventional (rules and regulations). (See also *Holland's Occupational Congruency Model.*)

Organizational Analysis is the first step in developing a strategic plan, which begins with the identification of the values critical to the organization.

Performance Gap Analysis identifies and describes past, present, and potential future human performance gaps.

Personality Inventory Instrument provides an accurate picture of a person's personality type and indicates personality preferences.

Personality Test is a less formal and less accurate version of a personality inventory instrument.

Psychodynamic Theory is a tool used to help predict career success, choice, and behavior by identifying what motivates individuals and the internal conflicts that exists in all human beings.

Reliability refers to the ability to repeat the same measurement in the same way over time.

Replacement Planning is a process to ensure the continuity of key leadership positions and the stability of tenure of an organization's personnel.

Roe's Theory of Occupation breaks occupations down into eight groups of service and six decision levels and is the basis for a number of tests to help determine best career choice based on interests.

Strategic Planning is the process that allows an organization to identify its aspirations and future challenges, clarify and gain consensus around a business strategy, communicate the strategy throughout the organization, align departments and personal goals with the overarching organizational strategy, and identify and align strategic initiatives. Often combined with long-term (five-to-ten year) planning initiatives, the process typically involves a strengths, weaknesses, opportunities, and threats (SWOT) analysis. (See also *SWOT.*)

Succession Planning is the process of identifying key positions, candidates, and employees to meet the challenges that an organization faces during change and over short-term and long-term timeframes.

Super Developmental Framework is a career development theory developed by D.E. Super based on the idea that careers move through five distinct phases from childhood through adulthood.

SWOT (Strengths, Weaknesses, Opportunities, and Threats) is an analysis tool used in strategic planning to establish environmental factors from within and outside an organization. (See also *Strategic Planning.*)

Task Analysis examines a single task within a job and breaks it down into the actual steps of performance.

Trait-And-Factor Counseling is the traditional approach to career decision making. Much of this approach came from Donald G. Paterson and later from E.G. Williamson.

Validity means measuring what the measurement instrument was intended to measure.

Workforce Plan identifies skill and knowledge gaps and the skills and knowledge required to meet future workforce needs. Additionally, it provides managers with a framework for making staffing decisions based on an organization's mission, strategic plan, budgetary resources, and a set of desired competencies.

Workforce Planning is the process and activities that ensure that an organization can meet its goals and objectives within a changing business environment. In other words, it ensures the right numbers of the right kinds of people are available at the right times and in the right place.

Appendix B
Answer Key

Chapter 1

1. Which of the following best defines strategic planning?

b. A process of systematically organizing the future

2. Which of the following best describes a subset of the correct strategic planning steps in the correct order?

a. Identification of organizational values, environmental analysis, identification of the organization's goals and objectives, identification of action steps designed to accomplish the plan

3. Workforce planning processes include which of the following steps?

b. Understand the business context, assess current realities, analyze gaps

4. Which of the following is not true?

d. Strategic planning identifies skill and knowledge gaps, and the skills and knowledge required to meet future workforce needs.

5. A workforce plan identifies

a. The skill and knowledge gaps and skills and knowledge required to meet future needs

6. Which of the following workforce planning processes is best described as determining future needs (performance, productivity, critical issues, and process improvements)?

b. Envisioning future needs

Chapter 2

1. A key difference between succession planning and replacement hiring is that succession planning is proactive and focuses on future needs, whereas replacement hiring is reactive to fill current positions.

a. True

2. Which of the following is not one of the approaches to replacement and succession planning?

c. Promoting

3. Which of the following is an example of an alternative job movement approach?

d. Outsourcing

4. Which of the following best describes competency modeling?

a. Identifying critical KSAs based on lists compiled by experts to identify the knowledge and breadth of skill that various managerial roles in the organization need

5. Which of the following is not a step in the succession planning process?

c. Identifying external factors

Chapter 3

1. A job analysis is the process of

b. Breaking a job into its component duty or functional areas

2. Two data-collection techniques used during job analysis are focus groups and corrective action reports.

a. True

3. Which of the following statements is not true?

b. A task analysis uses data-collection instruments that are quick and efficient to implement.

4. Which of the following is not usually conducted prior to conducting a job analysis?

d. Culture audit

5. Which of the following analysis methods uses a questionnaire, often with open-ended questions, when input is needed from employees and managers?

c. Surveys

6. Which of the following analysis methods is best used for processes with short-cycle jobs in production due to the time-consuming nature of this method?

b. Observation

7. All of the following are examples of job analyses except

d. Compensation analysis

8. All of the following are examples of job analysis outcomes except

a. Developing strategic plan goals

Chapter 4

1. Which of the following best describes Williamson's trait and factor theory?

b. People can be understood in terms of the characteristics they possess such as intelligence, ambition, aptitude, and self-esteem.

2. Which of the following best describes Ginzberg's theory?

a. Starting at the age of 18, people move from a career exploration to a series of events including educational specialization toward a specific career path and a final commitment to a career.

3. Which of the following best describes the Super developmental framework?

c. Careers move through five distinct phases from childhood through adulthood including growth, exploratory, establishment, maintenance, and decline stages.

4. The personality or typology theories of career development help explain the how and what of career choice.

a. True

5. Who is credited with the DECIDES model, a seven-step, decision-making process that provides a direct link between social learning theory, career development, and decision making?

a. Krumboltz

6. Which of the following is not an issue associated with career planning theories?

d. Organizational structure

7. Occupational counseling is a scientific approach to career decision making that leverages concepts from psychology.

b. False

8. Roe's theory of occupation is a tool used to predict career success, choice, and behavior by trying to understand what motivates individuals.

b. False

Chapter 5

1. Multi-rater feedback involves a process in which at least two levels of management review employees and agree on their candidacy for specific positions. Which of the following types of multi-rater feedback uses a questionnaire to ask superiors, direct reports, peers, and other internal and external customers how well an employee performs in a number of behavioral areas?

d. 360-degree feedback

2. Which of the following issues affects the development and administration of assessments and is concerned with the ability to repeat the same measurement in the same way over time?

a. Reliability

3. The ADA guarantees an individual with a disability the right to a job for which he or she is applying.

b. False

4. Which of the following is best described as one component of succession planning that identifies whether employees should stay in current positions or move to other positions?

d. Human resource audits

5. Assessment centers can contain a variety of exercises for employees to demonstrate skills through job-relevant situations.

a. True

6. Which of the following uses a four-dimensional model in an assessment, inventory, and survey format to indicate several characteristics, including dominance and optimism?

b. DiSC Personality Profile

7. Which of the following is concerned with measuring what was intended to be measured?

c. Validity

8. In the context of HRD, a decision to select someone to attend a training program is considered a test.

a. True

Chapter 7

1. All of the following are career counseling competencies except

d. Adult learning theory

2. All of the following are examples of career development models except

d. Career anchors

3. Career counseling is conducted by line managers and supervisors.

b. False

4. The primary goal of career guidance is to match an individual to a particular job or career path.

a. True

5. The primary issues facing web-based career counselors is/are

d. Establishing counselor-client relationships

Chapter 10

1. Which of the following is an example of an informal leadership development method?

d. Management and leadership self-study

2. Which of the following best describes the purpose of managerial leadership and development?

a. To affect organizational goals and objectives

3. All of the following are principles to guide strategic management development except

d. Subordinates are responsible for their own self-initiated learning and career development

4. In any organization, the following three principles hold true: each manager is responsible for his or her own development, executives are responsible for the development of their subordinates, and the organization is responsible for providing opportunities for the growth of all managers.

a. True

5. The managerial development process recognizes the fluidity of a manager's role, the differences in roles among different managerial levels, and different competency levels that these roles require.

a. True

6. The management development process is different from any other learning intervention.

b. False

Chapter 12

1. High-power-distance relationships are learner-oriented.

b. False

2. Which of the following space guidelines between adults is most appropriate for co-workers and social acquaintances (in the United States)?

c. Four to 12 feet

3. Proxemics refers to

b. Personal space

4. All of the following are strategies to create a diverse workforce except

d. Evaluation

5. The history and economic and political factors of a generation have no influence on the skills and abilities of those adults to learn.

b. False

6. Which of the following refers to a situation in which two individuals do not have a similar command of a language and may experience a misunderstanding because of mild distinctions between meanings of words?

d. Nuance errors

Chapter 13

1. All of the following are examples of resources used in career exploration except

d. Personality type indicators

2. A cross-functional job rotation is a formal program for international organizations in which managers or other employees are often assigned to a company department in another country.

b. False

3. Which of the following results from a comparison of individual strengths and weaknesses on the current job and individual potential for advancement to key positions in the future?

a. IDPs

4. Informational interviews are similar to job interviews in that a candidate applies for a particular job.

b. False

Appendix C
Index

ASTD Learning System Editorial Staff

Director: Cat Russo
Manager: Mark Morrow
Editors: Tora Estep, Jennifer Mitchell

Contributing Editors
April Davis, Stephanie Sussan

Proofreading
April Davis, Eva Kaplan-Leiserson

Graphic Design
Kathleen Schaner

ASTD (American Society for Training & Development) is the world's largest association dedicated to workplace learning and performance professionals. ASTD's 70,000 members and associates come from more than 100 countries and thousands of organizations--multinational corporations, medium-sized and small businesses, government, academia, consulting firms, and product and service suppliers.

ASTD marks its beginning in 1944 when the organization held its first annual conference. In recent years, ASTD has widened the industry's focus to connect learning and performance to measurable results, and is a sought-after voice on critical public policy issues.

Linking People, Learning & Performance

Thomson NETg Staff

Solutions Manager: Robyn Rickenbach
Director: John Pydyn

Contributing Writers
Lynn Lewis, Dawn Rader:

Contributing Editors
Lisa Lord, Kim Lindros, Karen Day

Thomson NETg is a global enterprise-learning leader offering an integrated suite of learning modalities and content, next generation technologies, and supportive strategic services designed to align with key organizational initiatives. NETg clients ensure continual, enterprise-wide acquisition of knowledge and information while lowering the overall cost of learning for the organization. With the KnowledgeNow Suite, clients are able to develop, customize, host, deliver, and report on engaging learning initiatives, delivered in blended modalities. Thousands of leading companies and government agencies around the world rely on Thomson NETg to achieve important business productivity and performance improvements. From healthcare to telecommunications, manufacturing to pharmaceuticals, retail to financial services, military operations to human services, NETg KnowledgeNow consistently delivers.

NETg is backed by The Thomson Corporation, a global enterprise comprised of a vast array of world-renowned publishing and information assets in the areas of academics, business and government, financial services, science and health care, and the law.